Changing Minds, If Not Hearts

AMERICAN GOVERNANCE: POLITICS,
POLICY, AND PUBLIC LAW

Series Editors
Richard Valelly, Pamela Brandwein,
Marie Gottschalk, Christopher Howard

A complete list of books in the series
is available from the publisher.

Changing Minds, If Not Hearts

Political Remedies for Racial Conflict

James M. Glaser

and

Timothy J. Ryan

PENN

UNIVERSITY OF PENNSYLVANIA PRESS

PHILADELPHIA

Published by
University of Pennsylvania Press
Philadelphia, Pennsylvania 19104-4112
www.upenn.edu/pennpress

Printed in the United States of America
on acid-free paper
10 9 8 7 6 5 4 3 2 1

Library of Congress Cataloging-in-Publication Data
Glaser, James M.
   Changing minds, if not hearts : political remedies for racial conflict /
James M. Glaser and Timothy J. Ryan.
      p. cm. — (American governance : politics, policy, and public law)
   Includes bibliographical references and index.
   ISBN 978-0-8122-4528-8 (hardcover : alk. paper)
   1. African-Americans—Political activity—21st century   2. African-
Americans—Politics and government—21st century.   3. Race—Political
aspects—United States—21st century.   4. Group identity—Political
aspects—United States—21st century.   5. Political participation—
United States—Psychological aspects.   6. United States—Race
relations—Political aspects.   I. Ryan, Timothy J.   II. Title.
III. Series: American governance.
   E185.615.G547 2013
   323.1196'0730905—dc23
                                                      2013005802

To Alison and Jared, with great love
and with confidence that you will contribute
to a more tolerant and peaceful world
—JMG

To Mom, for everything
—TJR

CONTENTS

CHAPTER 1

Burdens of Our Past

Ten weeks into a primary season that was supposed to last a month, victory must have seemed near, yet far. Barack Obama had outlasted veteran challengers for the Democratic presidential nomination and even held a delegate lead over his remaining opponent, Hillary Clinton. For a freshman senator to stand toe-to-toe with, and even edge out, Clinton's well-established political machine represented a remarkable feat of political acumen and grit. For Obama to do it signaled the tantalizing possibility that America had sufficiently shed the bonds of a past stained by racial strife so that a black man could win the nomination of a major party, and perhaps even the presidency.

In March, though, it was by no means a sure thing. Obama's delegate lead was narrow, and the largest of the eight states yet to vote was Clinton-friendly Pennsylvania. Michigan and Florida had held their elections on dates that violated Democratic Party rules, meaning delegates from those states (which had favored Clinton) were likely to be disqualified. But nobody was certain that the Democratic National Committee would really countermand the results of a popular election if they turned out to be pivotal. On top of it all, more than eight hundred party leaders, the so-called superdelegates, were free to vote independently and for the most part remained uncommitted, although many of them had been appointed to party positions by Clinton's husband in the 1990s.

It was in this setting that the Obama campaign confronted a crisis centered on race. To this point, Obama had followed the counsel that political strategists had given to Jane Byrne, vying to become the first female mayor of Chicago thirty years earlier: "You don't have to highlight what's already obvious" (quoted in Remnick 2008). Obama's campaign avoided appearances with polarizing blacks such as Al Sharpton and Jesse Jackson Sr. It focused on issues devoid of strong racial overtones—health care, Iraq, the economy. Where race came up explicitly, it was cast as a "metaphor for ambition" (Remnick 2008) and not—to the frustration of some black constituencies—in the spirit of recompense or grievance. To build and maintain a winning coalition of whites and blacks, Obama knew that he needed to carefully balance ownership of his race against the danger of letting it define his agenda.

Despite these efforts, race came to the center of attention, in two stages. First, on March 7, in an interview with the *Daily Breeze* (a Los Angeles–based newspaper), Geraldine Ferraro, a party stalwart and former Democratic vice presidential nominee, suggested that Obama benefited from being black: "If Obama was a white man, he would not be in this position. And if he was a woman (of any color) he would not be in this position. He happens to be very lucky to be who he is. And the country is caught up in the concept" (quoted in Farber 2008). Asked to apologize for her remarks, Ferraro instead dug in, telling the *New York Times* on March 12, "Every time that [Obama's campaign] is upset about something, they call it racist. . . . I will not be discriminated against because I'm white. If they think they're going to shut up Geraldine Ferraro with that kind of stuff, they don't know me" (quoted in Seelye 2008).

Ferraro's remarks proved to be a mere warm-up for what was to come the next day. On March 13, ABC's *Good Morning America* aired a disconcerting report on Obama's pastor of twenty years, the Reverend Jeremiah Wright. It was not the first time Wright had been a problem for the candidate. A year earlier, in a *Rolling Stone* article on Obama's background a number of inflammatory quotes by the minister had surfaced. Obama took steps to distance himself, saying Wright was "like an old uncle who says things I don't always agree with" (quoted in Ross 2008). But now, in sermons that would be played countless times on television and the Internet, millions of voters heard and saw Wright, who had officiated Obama's wedding and baptized his children, offer a racially charged harangue. The United States was the "US of KKK-A," he thundered, blaming Americans—white Americans— for a long train of plights new and old (Ross 2008). Questions arose about Obama's relationship to Wright, whom he had known for two decades, and Obama at once seemed as vulnerable as ever. As scrutiny continued to mount in the days following the report, his advisors remained outwardly cool, but they privately understood this as a "desperate fight for political survival" (Plouffe 2008, 204) and worried that "the wheels could easily spin off our whole venture" (Plouffe 2008, 210). Tellingly, Gallup's daily tracking poll showed that Obama's six-point advantage over Clinton as of March 13 became a seven-point deficit in the days after the Wright revelations (Gallup 2008).[1]

By the night of Friday, March 14, the campaign determined they needed a substantial response. Obama decided to give a landmark speech in which he would set the Wright controversy into the broader context of racial issues. The campaign had considered giving a speech on race back in the fall of 2007 to inoculate the candidate on the issue. Advisors David Axelrod and David Plouffe had objected, however, wanting to keep racial considerations submerged and not allow Obama to be thought of narrowly as the black candidate (Plouffe 2008, 211). Now, however, as perhaps was inevitable, it seemed imperative for Obama to define his vision of race relations in America. Working long after the campaign events of Saturday, Sunday, and Monday—advisors feared that cancelling them would suggest panic—Obama crafted a speech substantially by his own hand, e-mailing it to his staff at 2:00 A.M. Tuesday morning, about nine hours before he was to deliver it at Philadelphia's National Constitution Center (Wolffe 2009, 176).

The speech was a masterful exercise in the dismantling and reconstruction of a political issue. Obama did not distance himself from Wright, as would have been an obvious move. Rather, he took some ownership of the pastor's views, casting them as one instantiation of the negative impulses so many Americans feel in their hearts. Obama could "no more disown him [Wright] than I [could] my white grandmother—a woman who helped raise me, a woman who sacrificed again and again for me, a woman who loves me as much as she loves anything in this world, but a woman who once confessed her fear of black men who passed by her on the street, and who on more than one occasion has uttered racial or ethnic stereotypes that made me cringe." Obama noted with candor that the anger Wright expressed is common among blacks, in type if not degree: "The memories and humiliation and doubt and fear have not gone away; nor has the anger and the bitterness. . . . That anger may not get expressed in public in front of white co-workers or white friends. But it does find voice in the barbershop or around the kitchen table." At the same time, he articulated, with striking empathy and lucidity, the perceptions of competition and conflict that underpin many whites' feelings about issues of race:

In an era of stagnant wages and global competition, opportunity comes to be seen as a zero sum game, in which your dreams come at my expense. So when they [whites] are told to bus their children to a school across town; when they hear that an African American is getting an advantage in landing a good job or a spot in a good college because of an injustice that they themselves never committed; when they're told that their fears about crime in urban neighborhoods are somehow prejudiced, resentment builds over time.

Having acknowledged the problem and its significance, Obama continued with a redirection: would it be better to focus on Wright's comments and the cynicism that they evoked—the "burdens of our past"—or would it be better to focus on the many social and economic problems that Americans face together?

The speech quickly earned plaudits for its frankness, sophistication, and authenticity, with some commentators lavishing praise. Many others acknowledged the speech's quality, but were skeptical that it could defuse the potentially explosive situation. A *Time* article collecting reactions from political scientists and other experts reflected several gloomy assessments about Americans' ability to move past race. As one commented, "[Obama] is trying to take an actual position, rather than just distance himself from the Rev. Wright, who is clearly a political liability. But I think he is being naive. . . . A black candidate named Barack Hussein Obama can't have questions about his patriotism, and commitment to America, not if he is going to beat a genuine war hero. I think Obama is unelectable. He had to distance himself far from Wright. Instead, he was brave" (quoted in Newton-Small 2008). Others fretted that "the more he talks about race being unimportant or transcended, the more important it will become to the media and voters' perceptions," or that "while it [the speech] may convince some, there will inevitably be people out there who will not be able to disentangle Obama's words from Rev. Wright's" (quoted in Newton-Small 2008). *Wall Street Journal* columnist and former Reagan speechwriter Peggy Noonan praised Obama's message but vacillated on how effective it would be. We were in "unchartered territory," and "the speech will be labeled by history as the speech that saved a candidacy or the speech that helped do it in. I hope the former" (Noonan 2008).

With the benefit of hindsight, we know the speech was a success. The Wright controversy faded, Obama's polling numbers bounced back, and, for the first time, Americans embraced a black man as a major party nominee and, five months later, elected him.

We believe the Wright controversy and Obama's successful handling of it says something important about the way people think about race. It highlights that racial issues can draw the lines that divide political groups but also that these lines can dissolve and attention can focus on other matters, even while race remains in the background. It shows that race can divide, but that it need not do so. It illuminates the deep-seated feelings that come to bear when issues of race are at play, but also the potential to move beyond those feelings and not be governed by them. This is a book about that potential.

Race in the Abstract, Race in Practice

Americans have never been of one mind about race. African slaves came to the New World soon after the earliest European settlers, and objections to slavery are almost as old. Nearly a century before the American Revolution, for instance, Quaker settlers of Germantown, Pennsylvania, prepared a petition to their governing body arguing that holding slaves—allowable even among Quakers at the time—was inconsistent with Quaker doctrine and the progressive society they sought to create (Gerbner 2007). The American founders famously exhibited contradictions between the lofty egalitarian principles that justified revolt against the British king and their own practices. Writing the Declaration of Independence, Thomas Jefferson called the notion that all men were created equal "self-evident," and elsewhere he condemned slavery, calling it an "infamous practice," a "hideous blot," and asserting "nobody wishes more ardently to see an abolition not only of the trade but of the condition of slavery" (Jefferson 1788). Yet, like many of his contemporaries, Jefferson held slaves his whole life, and dozens of them were sold to pay debts upon his death (Finkelman 2001). In the Civil War, hundreds of thousands of northerners, led by an antislavery president, died to preserve the Union, but many of them exhibited the same unabashed racism as their southern counterparts. In the civil rights era, endorsement of equality started to become the norm, but an abiding commitment to states' rights became a workable rationale to justify the sharp disconnect between egalitarian principles and gross legal discrimination. When it comes to race in America, a gap between principles and practice is a persistent theme.

Today, there is still a stark contrast between the principles Americans endorse in the abstract and the actual condition of black Americans. Abstract egalitarianism is more entrenched than ever. In 2009, when the American

National Election Study asked a representative sample of 2,285 Americans whether the U.S. government should treat whites better than blacks, blacks better than whites, or both groups the same, 2,261 or fully 99 percent said both groups should be treated the same.[2] Similar proportions say that blacks should be as healthy as whites and should make the same amount of money as whites. Egalitarianism is taught in diversity-focused curricula, inculcated by children's shows like *Sesame Street*, and celebrated in thousands of multicultural clubs throughout the nation's colleges and universities. Inappropriate remarks—such as Trent Lott's 2002 statement that America would have had fewer problems if more people had voted for Strom Thurmond in 1948 (when Thurmond ran for president as a segregationist candidate)—are roundly denounced. And, of course, in 2008 America elected its first black president, a landmark that the *New York Times* characterized as "sweeping away the last racial barrier in American politics" (Nagourney 2008).

Yet, lurking below the surface, the inconsistencies remain. Obama's election indeed swept away a barrier, but there is substantial evidence that it did so not because egalitarianism washed racial antipathy away but rather because a combination of masterful tactics and sheer good luck allowed latent antipathy to be overcome. Political psychologists Michael Tesler and David O. Sears, for instance, show that Democratic voters who harbor negative feelings toward blacks substantially favored Hillary Clinton during the Democratic primaries—a striking pattern given how similar the candidates' platforms were (Tesler and Sears 2011, chap. 2). In the general election, the same measures of racial resentment appeared to predict voting against Obama, exerting far more influence—about three times as much—as in any presidential election since 1988, when the measures first became available (Tesler and Sears 2011, chap. 3). And although Obama's victory was decisive, it was not the landslide one could imagine. Donald Kinder and Allison Dale-Riddle examine what sort of election outcome one might have expected given the electoral climate. With an unpopular incumbent Republican presiding over two wars and an ailing economy, the models that political scientists have used to accurately predict election outcomes forecast that Obama would win the two-party vote by fourteen to eighteen percentage points, predictions that make Obama's actual victory of seven percentage points look rather meager. Absent race, Obama might well have won in a landslide. Absent an unpopular incumbent and an ailing economy, he might not have won at all (Kinder and Dale-Riddle 2011, chap. 4).

Looking still more broadly provides additional evidence that the endorsement of egalitarianism in the abstract is not fully implemented in the polling booth. The Voting Rights Act of 1965, as it has evolved, has prohibited the dilution of minority votes, a prohibition that subsequent litigation has determined applies to the drawing of congressional districts (Ansolabehere, Persily, and Stewart 2010). As a result, a number of "majority-minority" districts ensure that blacks hold a number of seats in the U.S. House of Representatives only a bit below their proportion of the population—forty-two seats (excluding nonvoting delegates) or 9.7 percent of the 112th Congress, compared to 12.6 percent of the U.S. population (Manning and Shogan 2011).[3] In contrast, there have been but six black senators throughout history, two of whom served during Reconstruction. The four in the modern era are Edward Brooke (1967–1979), Carol Moseley Braun (1993–1999), Barack Obama (2005–2008), and Roland Burris (2009–2010, by appointment). Thus, in the modern era, there has never been more than one at a time, and as we write there are none. Of twenty-six successful nominees to the Supreme Court since 1950, only two (7.7 percent) have been black (Thurgood Marshall and Clarence Thomas).

Things do not look much different when we turn our attention to the states. There have been well over seven hundred gubernatorial elections since 1950 but only three black governors: Douglas Wilder (governor of Virginia, 1990–1994), Deval Patrick (governor of Massachusetts, 2007–present), and David Paterson (governor of New York by succession, 2008–2010). State legislatures by and large also underrepresent blacks. When compared to the black proportion of the population in each state, data from the National Conference of State Legislatures (2009) give a sense of whether blacks are over- or underrepresented at the state level. If blacks constitute 15 percent of the population in a given state, for instance, do they hold 15 percent of the legislative seats? As Figure 1.1 shows, underrepresentation is much more common than overrepresentation. For lower chambers, in only five states (Michigan, Illinois, Ohio, Nevada, and California) are blacks overrepresented relative to their population. In the remaining forty-four they are underrepresented.[4] For upper chambers, the trend is much the same. Seven states overrepresent blacks, but they are underrepresented in forty-three others. In some cases, the underrepresentation is quite severe. In Louisiana, for instance, blacks constitute 32.7 percent of the population but hold only six of the thirty-nine state senate seats (15.8 percent). The underrepresentation is especially troubling in light of evidence that white legislators are less

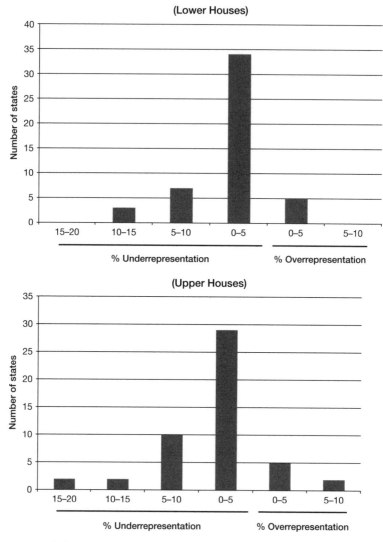

Figure 1.1. Black Over/Underrepresentation in State Legislatures
Source: National Conference of State Legislatures

responsive to identical requests that come from black citizens rather that white ones (Butler and Broockman 2011) and that both whites and blacks are more likely to contact representatives who share their race (Gay 2002). Moreover, as Zoltan Hajnal (2009) notes, taken together, these patterns mean that blacks, far more than whites or even Latinos or Asians, are likely to be "superlosers"—citizens who voted for losing candidates in all three (presidential, gubernatorial, and senatorial) elections.

Finally, despite general egalitarianism, the socioeconomic status of black Americans still represents, as Lawrence Bobo puts it, "the longest standing and most glaring exception to the American promise of freedom and equality" (Bobo 1988, 85). The differences are alarming and extend to every measure of well-being we can think of. Even if these are familiar, it is worth reflecting on how many disparities intersect. Compared to a non-Hispanic white child, a black child in America today is twice as likely to live below the poverty line (U.S. Census Bureau 2011), more than three times as likely to be born to a single parent, and more than twice as likely to have a low birth weight (Lin and Harris 2009). A representative black individual is about half as likely to have health insurance as a representative white one, and his or her family will have an income just 62 percent that of a white family (U.S. Census Bureau 2007). Even these disturbing differences understate the differences stemming from accumulated inequality—the inequality that emerges from whites' disproportionate benefit from inheritable assets such as stocks, bonds, homes, and so forth. One analysis finds that, at the turn of the century, the median black family had only ten cents for every dollar held by the median white family (Shapiro 2004). As we write these words, an updated analysis finds that this gap has expanded considerably as blacks were disproportionately hurt by the late-2000s financial crisis; as of 2009, the median white family held twenty times the wealth of the median black family (Kochhar, Fry, and Taylor 2011).

The differences extend beyond health and wealth. When it comes to education, blacks over the age of twenty-five are about half as likely as whites to hold an advanced degree and about twice as likely not to have finished a high school degree (U.S. Census Bureau 2010). Segregation of public schools now appears to be increasing. In the South, for instance, school integration exhibited a peak in 1988, when 43.5 percent of blacks attended majority-white schools. By 2005, this figure had decreased to 27 percent (Orfield and Lee 2007; see also Kozol 2005). Residential segregation has decreased over the years, but blacks remain the most segregated racial group in America

(Iceland, Weinberg, and Steinmetz 2002; Anderson 2010). As of 2001, 16.6 percent of black male adults had served time in prison, compared to only 2.6 percent of white male adults, a staggering discrepancy (Bonczar, 2003). In tandem with state disenfranchisement laws that last a lifetime in some cases, the result is that one in eight black males is ineligible to vote (Porter 2010). Blacks are also 70 percent more likely than whites to be victims of a violent crime (Truman and Rand 2010).

The intersection of so many disadvantages on one group is problematic not just for the people so hindered but for the political system as a whole. Pluralist democracy rests on the idea, expressed so elegantly by James Madison and his contemporaries, that although conflicts are inevitable, their ill effects will be made less severe to the extent the lines of conflict continually shift. Damage is brought under control and the system becomes more legitimate when the losers of today have the potential to be the winners of tomorrow. In contrast, as Robert Dahl notes, repeated losses exacerbate conflict: "If all the cleavages occur along the same lines, if the same people hold opposing positions in one dispute after another, then the severity of conflicts is likely to increase. The man on the other side is not just an opponent; he soon becomes an enemy" (Dahl 1967, 277).

Why, despite the general endorsement of egalitarianism, does the realization of full racial equality remain so distant? The question is broad and complex, encompassing an intricate convergence of multiple contributing factors, and no single study is likely to provide a fully satisfying answer. To be sure, part of an explanation comes from the legacy of oppression and marginalization of black communities in the United States. To sample but a small part of a vast literature, Thomas J. Sugrue (2005) conveys how decades of interpersonal and institutional discrimination coincided to leave urban blacks residentially segregated and impoverished (see also Bauman Biles, and Szylvian 2000; Hirsch 1983), while Ira Katznelson (2006) illuminates racial considerations that steered New Deal aid projects to aid whites at the expense of blacks. Even today, many argue that many distributive and criminal justice policies work to the disadvantage of blacks (e.g., Provine 2007). A number of studies (e.g., Bertrand and Mullainathan 2004) persuasively demonstrate that discrimination in the private sphere still makes it particularly difficult for blacks to obtain jobs that might break the cycle of poverty. At the same time, although such studies are occasionally painted as "blaming the victim," it would be foolish to dismiss evidence that underdeveloped human capital (Heckman and Krueger 2004) or dysfunctional cultural norms

(Wilson 2010) in the black community have a reciprocal relationship with the discriminatory patterns.

As political scientists and students of public opinion, our interest—as well as our comparative advantage—is to explore the psychological tendencies that influence political outcomes: are there factors that regularly work against blacks' ability to win in majoritarian politics? Are there factors that cause them to lose in the game of politics, or at least to get less of, "who gets what, when, and how," to use Harold Lasswell's famous phrasing (Lasswell 1950)? We argue that there are. Specifically, we contend that whites have a proclivity to understand choices—especially choices that arise when blacks raise grievances or call for redress—as presenting a conflict of group interests. When that interpretation arises, whites tend to oppose options that require concessions. This pattern undermines support for a host of policies designed to address the inequalities described above. By presenting evidence for these ideas, our goal is not to explain the whole of economic, social, or even political inequality. What we hope, rather, is to illuminate one important feature of the American political environment that systematically works against blacks, lessening the protections that pluralism and the division of power are meant to provide.

Our thesis is that, although politics is part of the problem, it also may contain the seeds of a solution. When it comes to organizing thoughts about politics, group interests have a head start relative to other considerations, but that does not mean that they need always prevail. One of the most consistent findings in psychology is that the human mind employs a plethora of tools, each active in different contexts, to make sense of and respond to a complex reality (Cosmides and Tooby 1994). Some of these tools countervail the desire to protect one's in-group, and politics—the right sort of politics— can help bring them to bear.

In the pages that follow, we lay the groundwork for our argument. First, we review some insights from the psychology of opinion formation. We describe evidence that the opinions people express when they respond to a survey or even when they enter a voting booth are not fixed and stable, as we often think of them, but rather are a complex amalgamation of different considerations, both cognitive and emotional, with different considerations taking precedence under different circumstances. Second, with this framework in hand, we discuss which considerations take precedence when people think about race. We argue that the predominant framework is one of *group conflict*, a mentality in which the interests of different racial groups are seen as being at odds with each other. This pattern of thinking leads whites to oppose many policies that blacks favor. Or, as Obama put it, white resistance is generated where the perception is that blacks' dreams come at whites' expense. We argue that the tendency is not irrepressible, that the tools of politics can change the way people think about racial issues.

Forming Opinions Is a Process

It is common to think and talk about political opinions as though they were fixed, a set of stable ideas we carry around in our brain like slips of paper in a catalogue, ready to be accessed when the situation—a conversation with a friend or question from a pollster, for instance—calls for it. In this view, expressing an opinion is a simple act of retrieval; if the pollster asks whether we favor or oppose increased spending on Social Security, we retrieve the Social Security slip and express what is written on it. If we learn new facts that cause us to change the opinion, we access the slip, erase what was written on it, write something new, and file it away again. This way of thinking is at play when television commentators make a statement like "Fifty-six percent of Americans think Social Security spending should increase." The implication is that fifty-six out of every hundred people walking around happen to have "favor" slips filed away in their respective catalogues.[5]

The "catalogue" model of opinions makes some intuitive sense. It is consistent with the impression that our own opinions have some stability to them, that we are accessing something quite deep and considered when we express an opinion. It also seems like an important part of what civics lessons teach about the democratic process—that the majority opinion carries special weight because it means that, through contemplation and life experience, more people filed away slips that said one thing rather than another.

Unfortunately, in most cases, there is no catalogue. Myriad studies show that few people live up to the image of a highly engaged, contemplative citizen who knows and has thought about the issues of the day. Indeed many people go through their lives thinking about politics hardly at all. Even when circumstances require attention to politics—such as when people are presented with an election—the decision is often between just two choices, not the sort of task that requires deep, well-formed opinions about the wide array of issues that politics can engage. Thus, when people are called upon to express an opinion about an issue, the response, typically, is as much an act of construction—one that occurs quickly and on the fly—as one of retrieval. The words people speak, or the ballot choice they mark, is the outcome of an intricate process in which bits of information encoded in memory are accessed, processed, and reconciled (cf. Zaller 1992).

The evidence for this model is abundant. We see it in the plentiful psychological work on what is known as *framing*, the construction of choices to elicit particular considerations (Gamson and Modigliani 1987). The canonical demonstration of framing effects comes from an experiment run by Amos Tversky and Daniel Kahneman in 1981. Tversky and Kahneman asked subjects which of two treatments for a rare disease they would favor. The two choices presented a trade-off between risk and reward, as one would save a few lives with certainty, but the other could save either everyone or no one with some probability. For some subjects, the choices were described in terms of how many lives would be saved. For other subjects, they were described in terms of how many people would die, but either way, the choices were mathematically and logically equivalent. Still, subjects in the experiment (in a result that has been replicated many times) were much more prone to choose the risky option when it was framed in terms of avoiding deaths than when framed as saving lives. It seems that, psychologically, losses loom larger than gains. More broadly, the demonstration shows that preferences stem in large part from which situational features are salient.

It is easy to see why framing would happen often in politics and why it would behoove politicians to think carefully about which frames will generate support for their agenda. Ask Americans whether the government spends too little on "welfare" and just over 20 percent say yes, but ask them whether too little is spent on "assistance to the poor" and more than 60 percent say yes (Rasinski 1981). Ask them whether a hate group should be allowed to hold a political rally and you can increase support from 45 percent to 85 percent if you say, "given the importance of free speech" rather than "given the risk of violence" (Sniderman and Theriault 2004). Indeed, politicians frame issues ubiquitously and reflexively. Depending on who is doing the framing, tax expenditures can be either "corporate handouts" or "incentives to create jobs." Fiscal austerity can be called "balancing the budget" or "cutting programs."

One task of public opinion scholarship, then, is to understand the nature of public opinions and how they relate to political outcomes. Which opinions come to bear under different circumstances? Which ones reflect cognizance of the consequences of different alternatives? Which ones are open to change due to presentation, choice structure, and discourse? Which ones would change if people knew more? What institutional rules transform opinions of the people—which may or may not be reasoned, principled, fair, just, and forward looking—into political outcomes that are?[6]

If we are to begin to make sense of these questions in the domain of race politics, we will need to know something about which frames guide thinking about race. The next section reviews evidence showing that a critical framework that comes to mind is one of group conflict.

Group Conflict

In 1954, psychologist Muzafer Sherif and colleagues arranged for school-boys aged eleven and twelve to visit an isolated summer camp near Robbers Cave in Oklahoma. Prior to the experiment, the researchers gave the boys personality tests, observed them, and interviewed their families and teachers to ensure that they were all fairly similar and well adjusted. They were all white, Protestant, and middle-class. Then, without having met each other, they were divided into two groups of a dozen each and brought to the camp separately.

For the first several days, the two groups lived in separate areas and did not know of each other's existence. They hiked, camped, cooked, and played together, developing social bonds and an esprit de corps. They gave themselves names—one group dubbed itself the Eagles, the other the Rattlers—and each group's members grew to know the distinct personalities and talents of others in the group.

Next, the counselors brought the two groups together under conditions of conflict. They arranged competitive games of baseball, touch football, and tug-of-war. Although amicable at first, hostility soon developed. One group accused the other of cheating and both started to call the other demeaning names. As Sherif recounts, "The rival groups made threatening posters and planned raids, collecting secret hoards of apples for ammunition.... The Eagles, after a defeat in a tournament game, burned a banner left behind by the Rattlers; the next morning the Rattlers seized the Eagles' flag when they arrived on the athletic field. From that time on name-calling, scuffles and raids were the rule of the day" (Sherif 1956, 57). Later, social events, such as the opportunity for the two groups to come together for a meal, "served as opportunities for the rival groups to berate and attack each other. In the dining-hall line they shoved each other aside, and the group that lost the contest for the head of the line shouted 'Ladies first!' at the winner. They threw paper, food, and vile names at each other at the tables. An Eagle bumped by a Rattler was admonished by his fellow Eagles to brush 'the dirt' off his clothes" (Sherif 1956, 57–58). In short, the conflictual conditions the researchers artificially established served to engender hostility between groups, even though the groups were, by design, quite similar and had no predisposition for animosity.

The Robbers Cave experiments are remembered because they are a vivid illustration of an endemic human proclivity. The proclivity is for people, cognizant of the social groups to which they belong, to see the world through a groupcentric lens. This is especially the case for decisions about the allocation of privileges and scarce resources. Where alternatives are seen in a zero-sum context, perceptions of threat arise, and individuals are likely to favor options that they perceive as protecting their group's interests. When focused on a conflict of interests, any negative feelings toward an out-group that an individual might harbor are especially likely to come to bear. Conflict, as Gordon Allport put it, sets "all prejudices that are attuned to it into simultaneous vibration" (1954, 233).

The group conflict mind-set is all the more troubling in light of evidence that group classifications arise organically, perhaps even irrepressibly. Henri Tajfel and colleagues demonstrated as much in a series of famous "minimal group" experiments. In one such experiment (Tajfel et al. 1971), subjects were brought into a lab to watch a series of images full of dots flash on a screen for a fraction of a second each (far too little time to count). After each image, subjects estimated how many dots were on the screen. At the end of the sequence, the estimates were (ostensibly) analyzed and each subject was told that he was either the kind of person who consistently overestimates the number of dots, or the kind of person who consistently underestimates them. In reality, the subjects' estimates had no bearing on how the experimenter classified them. Rather, the labels were assigned purely at random. The idea was to construct a completely arbitrary classification, one with no history, no basis in previously existing attitudes, and no rational relationship to individual interests.

How did subjects respond to this entirely artificial (one might say downright silly) classification? It became real and significant. In the series of tasks that followed, subjects were invited to assign monetary rewards and penalties to the other participants in the experiment. This phase took place immediately after the group assignment, so social interactions could not have caused subjects to like the people in their in-group more. Still, the in-group—an in-group that a few minutes earlier did not exist—was clearly favored. Numerous follow-up studies replicated the pattern of results, some showing it even more starkly. In one study, subjects were explicitly told that groups would be assigned on the basis of a coin flip. Even when subjects knew that the assignment was due to chance, they showed the same pattern of preferential behavior (Billig and Tajfel 1973).

There is reason to expect racial classifications to be particularly powerful in shaping group perception. When psychologists measure how individuals classify the people they meet, they find race to be one of the three "primitive" categories (the other two being age and sex) that the brain encodes in almost every social interaction (Hewstone, Hantzi, and Johnston 1991; Brewer 1988; Stangor et al. 1992; Kurzban, Tooby, and Cosmides 2001). Thus, while one might not attend to the hair color or eye color of someone we have just met, we will almost certainly take account of her race. A late-night comedian's claim that he does not see race ("People tell me I'm white and I believe them because I own a lot of Jimmy Buffett albums") is funny precisely because our own experiences make it so implausible. While the minimal group studies "created" social categories, there is reason to believe that race operates to categorize people, perhaps with similar discriminatory effect, in all manner of social interactions. And of course race, particularly the cleavage between blacks and whites, has been a focus of many of the most significant political conflicts throughout U.S. history.

In politics, instances of group conflict abound. Group conflict theory explains why major obstructionist efforts would arise just as major legislation seeks to revise majority-group privileges (Burstein 1979) and why whites exhibit considerably more aversion to sending their children to integrated schools when the school is majority black, where black interests and values are better represented, than when it is majority white (Smith 1981). It is in keeping with evidence that Americans are more opposed to immigration in places where immigrants might drain state fiscal resources than in other places (Hainmueller and Hiscox 2010) and that Americans are especially opposed to immigration from dissimilar out-groups, even when the level of threat is held constant (Brader, Valentino, and Suhay 2008).[7]

In American politics, a canonical demonstration of group conflict dynamics comes from V. O. Key's analysis of the American South, which concluded that the orientation toward white supremacy took deepest root in the so-called Black Belt, the agricultural region where the soil was richest, where plantation agriculture was most likely to take hold, where the demographic legacy of slavery was strongest, and where blacks thus constituted the highest proportion of the population. As Key (1949, 5) writes, "It is the whites of the black belts who have the deepest and most immediate concern about the maintenance of white supremacy. Those whites who live in counties with populations 40, 50, 60, and even 80 percent Negro share a common attitude toward the Negro." Key's conclusion received support from a number of analyses of census and polling data (Giles 1977; Wright 1977; Glaser 1994; Bobo and Hutchings 1996). We have generated additional contemporary experimental evidence that supports Key's insights.[8] In a telephone survey, we asked a random sample of adults to imagine a hypothetical state and to think about whether it should draw the borders of its congressional districts so as to ensure that blacks would be elected to a number of seats proportional to their population. (As the reader may recognize, the setup was inspired by disputes over the construction of "majority-minority" districts, where minority candidates are likely to win; e.g., *Bush v. Vera*, 517 U.S. 952, 1996.) The hypothetical state, however, was described differently to different respondents. Some were told it was only 10 percent black. Others were told it was 25, 40, or even 55 percent black. Thus, the question script read:

> As you may know, congressional representatives are elected in districts. How these districts are drawn by state officials has been controversial. The controversy is over the practice of drawing district lines for the purpose of making sure that candidates from underrepresented groups get elected. Think about a state where blacks make up [10/25/40/55] percent of the population. How do you think this state's district lines should be drawn? Do you think the districts should be drawn to guarantee that roughly [percentage as from above] percent of the elected representatives are black, or do you think that the lines should be drawn without regard to who will get elected?

Our conjecture was that as blacks became a larger and more formidable political entity (even just hypothetically), white respondents would become more opposed to their interests.

Table 1.1 shows how changing the racial makeup of the hypothetical state affected whites' responses. When the state is only 10 percent black, 22.8 percent of whites support guaranteed representation—a small but not trivial proportion. With each step increase in blacks' proportion of the population,

Table 1.1. Group Conflict at Work

					Significance
Racial districting experiment					
	10% black state	25% black state	40% black state	55% black state	
Percent guaranteeing representation	22.8 (136)	22.5 (102)	16.1 (93)	14.3 (112)	.05*
Municipal jobs experiment					
	10% black city	30% black city	50% black city		
Percent guaranteeing set-asides	16.9 (136)	12.1 (132)	7.0 (114)		.01**
City contracts experiment					
	10% black city	25% black city	40% black city	55% black city	
Percent guaranteeing representation	12.4 (210)	9.9 (233)	6.2 (241)	9.2 (228)	.13

* p < .10   ** p < .05

Source: 1998–1999 Multi-investigator study.

Notes: Numbers in parentheses represent the number of subjects assigned to each condition. Significance test is for the coefficient in a logistic regression in which the (randomized) percentage black is the independent variable and support for the provision is the dichotomous dependent variable.

white support decreases, perhaps with something of a tipping point coming between 25 and 40 percent (well before blacks constitute a majority, we note). Statistical analysis confirms that these differences almost certainly do not arise just due to chance variation; the whites in the sample really did become less accommodating in step with the hypothetical proportion of blacks. The same pattern emerges in a similar experiment in which respondents are asked about the distribution of municipal jobs (row 2 of Table 1.1) or city contracts (row three) in a hypothetical city. The experiment shows that the psychology of power dynamics has a clear and consequential impact on thinking about politics in these domains.

The literature on group conflict, prodigious and growing, has almost entirely focused on the politics of tangible resources like political representation, municipal jobs, city contracts, green cards and citizenship papers, and seats in universities. Given that these tend to be zero-sum issues where more to members of one group means less for members of another, it is little wonder that they evoke competitive attitudes. But group conflict thinking may not stop there. In these pages, we aim to extend the group conflict argument and argue that the clash of interests within the political realm goes beyond how economic, educational, and political goods are distributed.

Many of the most contentious racial issues are actually not about resources but about symbols. Consider some of the racial issues that have dominated headlines over the past few decades. How do we recognize civil rights heroes like Martin Luther King Jr. and Rosa Parks? Should Confederate flags wave from public spaces? Should the government and society apologize for past wrongs? Should the president's cabinet or the Supreme Court "look like America"? What are the limits of dialogue on issues of race and ethnicity (and gender and sexual orientation), and how "politically correct" must our conversations be? These are not issues that would tend to make a difference to anyone's livelihood or life span. Nevertheless, they matter. They matter deeply because they broach the very essence of group membership. They matter broadly because unlike economic issues, which affect only some in the group, these issues can be perceived as personal by almost all in the group. And so political processes engage these symbolic issues and allow us to allocate things that are generally difficult to allocate, like heritage, respect, legitimacy, responsibility, and moral high ground. Group conflict defines some of these battles over symbols, and they can be understood, we argue, much like battles over economic or political resources.

The dynamic that arises when groups compete over economic, political, or symbolic resources seems all the more distinctive when we consider it against the background of a substantial psychological literature on what is known as the "contact hypothesis." The contact hypothesis, as Allport (1954, 255) states it, expects that when members of different groups become acquainted with each other through regular interaction, it "is likely to engender sounder beliefs concerning minority groups, and for this reason contribute to the reduction of prejudice." In other words, as stereotypes are disconfirmed and as members of out-groups become individualized, hostility should decrease. There is abundant evidence in favor of the contact hypothesis (cf. Carsey 1995; Pettigrew and Tropp 2006; Green and Wong 2009), but in its simplest form its expectations diverge with those of group conflict theory. Consider that it might predict whites living in the black belt to be most sympathetic to black interests, since, with blacks constituting such a large part of the population, the two groups would have many occasions to interact. That the whites who live in these areas appear most hostile to blacks' interests (Fossett and Kiecult 1989; Glaser 1994) calls attention to the effects of different kinds of interaction. Proximity can and often does breed liking and cohesion. When it occurs under conditions of competition, however, it does quite the opposite.

Hearts and Minds

Group conflict theory's most notable feature is its emphasis on the circumstantial nature of racial conflicts. Hostility, it says, comes from scarce resources and clashing interests. Reasonable readers might ask if there is not something missing from this perspective. What about racism as an individual disposition? What about feelings of resentment, dislike, disgust, or even hatred directed at members of out-groups? How much do these underlying sentiments influence opinions and behavior?

The question is difficult to answer because the sentiments themselves are difficult to measure. People likely do not have fully conscious access to the feelings that govern their behavior (Dutton and Aron 1974; Nisbett and Wilson 1977; Kurzban and Aktipis 2007). Even if they did, there now is social desirability pressure against reporting prejudiced feelings. Still, social scientists have spent much time and energy devising ways to measure racial feelings and their impact. Here, we briefly review two notable approaches.

The first approach uses survey questions that attempt to tap feelings of racial antipathy indirectly. There are numerous variations on this theme, including scales that measure "modern racism," "symbolic racism," "racial resentment," "subtle prejudice," and others (see Kinder forthcoming for a review), and the exact instrumentation has changed over time. The common approach, however, is to present subjects with statements that let them express negative feelings toward blacks (or other minorities) while still endorsing egalitarian principles. A typical statement is, "Irish, Italian, Jewish and many other minorities overcame prejudice and worked their way up. Blacks should do the same without any special favors." An individual does not need to harbor negative feelings toward blacks to endorse such a statement. At the same time, the endorsement is more likely to the extent such feelings exist. Measured this way, it appears that many whites do harbor negative feelings toward blacks. These feelings appear, above and beyond ideology, partisanship, and several other measures, to predict attitudes toward racially sensitive policies such as affirmative action (Kinder and Sanders 1996), as well as voting against Obama in both primary and general elections (Kinder and Dale-Riddle 2011).

The second approach, which is more recent, is to tap so-called implicit attitudes, "traces of past experience that mediate favorable or unfavorable feeling, thought, or action toward an object" (Banaji 2001, 122). The idea here is that a person could harbor latent positive or negative associations toward racial groups that, even if not endorsed or consciously accessible, still impact behavior. In one approach to measuring such associations, researchers use a computer to time how quickly subjects can sort images of white and black faces into positive and negative categories, examining whether the subjects find it easier to make associations between white faces and positive words like "wonderful," "beautiful," and so on, than to associate black faces with these words.[9] Many do. On average, white respondents take one-fifth of a second longer to associate black faces with positive words and white faces with negative words than vice versa. Moreover, the strength of this bias appears to relate to explicit measures of prejudice, as well as behavior, such as visible discomfort around blacks and evaluations of an essay ostensibly written by a black student (Greenwald et al. 2009; Fazio and Olson 2003). There is also some evidence that negative implicit attitudes toward blacks decreased support for Barack Obama in the 2008 election (Pasek et al. 2009; Payne et al. 2010).

Measuring feelings, especially stigmatic or unconscious ones, is a messy business, and these approaches, it should come as no surprise, have their critics with respect to both conception and measurement (e.g., Sniderman and Tetlock 1986; Arkes and Tetlock 2004). We do not venture into the debate here but note that citizens' personal traits continue to be a focal point in the study of race and politics. For instance, one recent study argues that Americans' opinions about health care reform became firmly moored in racial sentiments as the issue became more and more associated with Barack Obama (e.g., Tesler 2012).

We think such debate is worthwhile and proper but leaves out something important and practical. Our discussion of framing characterized opinion construction as a process in which different considerations, perhaps many of them, are brought to bear. Often, it is a fickle process in which subtly calling to mind different priorities or ways of making sense of an issue make large differences in the opinions people express. Our conjecture is that the stew of politics, where interests collide, resources are limited, and antagonism often succeeds, provides a rich environment for group conflict thinking to blossom. On the other hand, perhaps there are ingredients that can neutralize the solution—if not changing the underlying sentiments, at least making it less likely that they will come to bear. Perhaps the Achilles' heel of racial animus, in other words, is its contingent nature. Kinder (1998, 807) states the idea elegantly:

> Group-centrism provides a powerful and compelling logic for public opinion, but there is nothing inevitable or universal about it. . . . [It] will be a more or less prominent feature of American public opinion depending on the particular constellation of issues temporarily holding center stage. Furthermore, public issues are multifaceted: they are always "many issues at once" (Verba et al., 1987, 94). A proposal for national health care might be understood as help for the working poor, or as an unwelcome intrusion of the federal government, or as a solution to one's own health care needs. Group-centrism is prominent in the first interpretation but invisible in the other two. Thus what may seem to be a natural mode of political thinking in fact is not natural: group-centrism depends on how citizens understand issues, which in turn depends on how issues are framed in elite debate. (Kinder 1998, 807)

When it comes to race, the hunch that we might be able change minds even without changing hearts is, in many ways, optimistic. Patterns of thought can and do change as arguments are won, norms evolve, new principles take hold, and education improves. Sentiments, in contrast, are difficult to change. Consider how the landscape of public opinion has evolved since the start of the civil rights movement. Fifty years ago, substantial proportions of Americans explicitly opposed the integration of public schools, desegregated transportation, equal access to public spaces like parks and restaurants, and the ability of blacks to live in white neighborhoods. By the 1990s, open opposition to these measures had softened to a whisper (Schuman et al. 1998); pollsters, for the most part, stopped routinely asking such questions for lack of meaningful variation. New issues have, of course arisen, but this particular turf is no longer contested. Figure 1.2 shows two representative trends in white opinions, one for a question asking whether whites and blacks should go to the same schools, the other asking whether white people have a right to keep blacks out of their neighborhoods if they want to (Schuman et al. 1998).

Did this sea change of opinion stem from changes in how whites feel toward blacks? Not by one reasonable measure. Since 1964, the American National Election Study—a benchmark national survey conducted every presidential election year—has used a survey instrument called the feeling thermometer to ask a representative sample of whites how they feel toward various groups, including blacks. Respondents choose a value between zero and 100, with higher values indicating great warmth and 50 demarcating a neutral feeling.

The solid dark line in Figure 1.2 shows how whites have responded to the feeling thermometer over time. Its most notable feature is its stability.[10] In 1964, at the height of the civil rights movement, just five months after passage of the Civil Rights Act of 1964, the average response was 60.7. In 2008, just after Obama's election, it was 66.0; in fifty-four years it moved just over 5 points, less than 1 per decade, a rate far outpaced by the change in opinion about specific policies. (As shown in the figure, opinion on the residency question moves 47 points in thirty-three years.) The same stability is not evident for all groups. As Figure 1.2 shows, feelings toward gays and lesbians increased four times as much in roughly half the interval.[11]

Underlying feelings toward groups are important and many attempts to change them are admirable. But when it comes to the outcomes of majoritarian politics, what matters is the choices people make in a few pivotal moments: when they enter the voting booth, when they are called by a pollster, when they discuss political issues with friends and family. Clearly

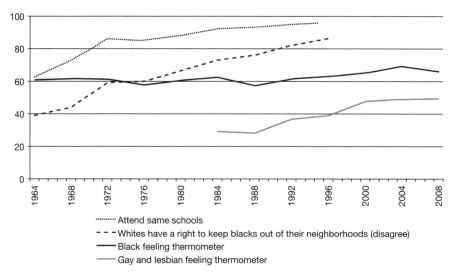

Figure 1.2. Opinions Change; Sentiments Stay the Same
Source: American National Election Study cumulative file. Figure shows weighted means for
each year.

feelings can influence these choices, but psychology tells us that perhaps
they need not. Perhaps it is possible to change minds, if not hearts.

An Experimental Approach

We have argued that policy opinions, including those expressed in surveys
and elections, are the end result of a process and that to assess the political
outcomes they generate, we need to think about whether process is stable and
robust, or sensitive to arbitrary features of presentation and framing. How
will we know?

In recent years, we began to experiment with an approach—one unusual
in our discipline—intended to strengthen the bridge between abstract academic theorizing and political confrontations as they happen "on the ground."
We kept a sharp lookout for real instances of racially charged conflict, which
unfortunately were not hard to find. When they emerged, we asked, first,
what aspects of the situation might be energizing group conflict and, second,
might it be possible to recast the issue in a way that would keep the proclivity
inert? We then devised studies that focused a lens on the psychological

mechanisms at play, mirroring the crucial circumstances and testing how people would respond to alternative presentations of the same dilemma. By using geographically compact samples and conducting our tests during or shortly after the conflict in question, we were able to focus attention on the very people who gave rise to and experienced the confrontation. In many cases, we show that group conflict thinking matters deeply for conflicts in the real world. When we reframe political choices so as to disarm its triggers, the very same people who exhibited intransigence and hostility become far more moderate, empathetic, and accommodating.

The topical and geographical variety of where we conduct our studies speaks to group conflict's broad significance; it is not particular to a single issue or locality. Our investigations take us first to a traditional "dollars and cents" confrontation in Jackson, Mississippi, where for years the city's voters defeated ballot initiatives to fund the overwhelmingly black public schools (Chapter 2). The next two chapters focus on some of the "symbolic" issues we allude to above, issues where material interests take a back seat to the emotions tied up in gestures and principles. We visit Columbia, South Carolina, where black voters lobbied, to the consternation of many whites, to remove the Confederate flag from the state capitol building (Chapter 3). Chapter 4 takes us to Oklahoma, where blacks devastated by the Tulsa Race Riot of 1921 asked, in their old age, that restitution and apology for the white government's complicity finally be made. Chapters 5 and 6 present a two-pronged investigation of affirmative action in college admissions. First we go to Michigan and examine how opinions about affirmative action change when we call attention to other preferences that exist in the admissions process. Next, we explore two sides of the principle of race neutrality—its application to conflicts in California and New Jersey.

We mean "an experimental approach" as a double entendre in that it refers not just to the flexibility we cultivate but also to our favorite scientific tool. All of our studies incorporate, in some way, randomized experiments on public opinion surveys. Randomized experiments, long common in psychology and medical research, have only recently come into their own in political science (Druckman et al. 2006, 2011). In randomized experiments, individuals are assigned to separate groups that are then, in some way, treated differently. For medical researchers, this usually means they are given different drugs (and placebos). For laboratory psychologists, it often means the experimenter interacts with lab subjects differently; we have already seen this in Tajfel's minimal group experiments, where researchers divided subjects into overestimators and underestimators. Our experiments steer respondents to think about our issues of interest in different ways. We call attention to alternative considerations, frame debates differently, and present respondents with different choices to see how opinions respond.

The essence of randomized experiments, including ours, is that subjects are assigned to different conditions purely by chance. This simple operation solves a profound problem. Human behavior is subject to so many complexities and foibles that it is very difficult to identify the effect of a particular cause amidst all the noise (cf. Holland 1986). If one distributes Democratic campaign leaflets in one neighborhood, for example, and the people who live there exhibit greater support for the Democratic candidate than people in a different neighborhood, is it because the leaflets worked, or because the neighborhood was more attractive to Democrats in the first place? By assigning the treatment purely by chance, one has good reason to believe that difference of interest has been isolated. Moreover, the statistical adjustments that researchers often apply to identify causal effects—adjustments that have fallen under increased scrutiny in recent years (Freedman 2008; Mutz 2011)—are unnecessary.

Political scientists employ all sorts of experiments, including ones conducted in a lab, in the field, or even over the airwaves (Panagopoulos and Green 2008). We embed our experiments in public opinion surveys, the sort of surveys that news outlets like *Newsweek* routinely conduct, splitting the respondents into two or more comparable groups and asking each a different form of a question. This sort of approach began as a way for researchers to better understand their survey instruments.[12] For instance, in one classic study, researchers wondered whether American respondents would be more likely to say that the United States should admit reporters from Communist countries if they previously had been asked whether Communist countries should admit reporters from the United States (indeed, support went up dramatically) (Hyman and Sheatsley 1950). Scholars soon realized, however, that survey experiments, artfully crafted, could answer substantive questions as well. By subtly calling attention to some considerations or others and comparing the thought processes that emerged, researchers could trace the psychology underlying citizens' attitudes about a host of topics. And they could do so with greater confidence in the external validity of their findings because the surveys can employ a variety of tools (such as random-digit dialing) to recruit a representative sample of a population. Paul Sniderman and Thomas Piazza (1993, 11–12), whose creative use of the survey experiment brought new insight to the study of race, write that the method combines "the advantages of experimental design and the standard representative sample" to "expose aspects of the thinking about race always before in the shadows." They also argue that the technique gives new perspective on the flexibility of some racial attitudes and the "potential for change in racial politics [that] has gone virtually unsuspected—and certainly understudied" (10).

Our experiments follow a common pattern. We start from the premise that, because the episodes we study center on conflictual political issues, they are likely to be colored by group conflict considerations. Whites, that is, are likely to view our issues through a competitive lens, increasing motivation to protect resources or privileges. The experimental treatments we employ test ways of reframing issues to direct attention away from these considerations. Is group conflict inextricably tied to the issues at hand, or can we interrupt group conflict impulses by recasting an issue and calling attention to alternative ways of thinking about it?

We are particularly concerned with realism. If we can demonstrate that it is possible to interrupt the group conflict pattern of thinking and change public opinion about racial issues, the demonstration will be all the more compelling to the extent it can be replicated by real actions. Thus, we do not rely on convenience samples (e.g., college students and airport travelers), as is often done, but representative samples of citizens in our areas of brewing racial controversy. Further, our experiments mimic political tools that actors can employ and have employed. We use rhetorical devices that put a different face on a decision. We restructure political choices (an art William Riker [1986] calls "heresthetics") to see if they lead to different outcomes. In many different places we successfully move the public, even transforming a minority opinion to a majority opinion in some cases.

What does it mean to change opinions in this way? Some might object that doing so is manipulative. Perhaps it uses trickery to adulterate a pure view of what people believe. We disagree. The attitudes that find expression in our experiments are no less genuine or real than others. Rather, we are unpacking the process by which the multifaceted attitudes that lie below the surface are given voice—not only what people think about political issues but how they have gotten to their positions. Our results should lead to a thoughtful discussion about how government should account for the different facets of opinion in constructing policy. We shall have more to say about this in the conclusion.

Our experiments are somewhat distinctive within political science. When political scientists field survey experiments, they often take the form of large, expensive, omnibus studies designed to test a slate of ideas and hypotheses. This is a practical way to proceed, as the expense of conducting one survey, much less two or more surveys, is substantial. Researchers find it pragmatic because it offers the opportunity to test many different hypotheses at one time. As we note above, our approach, in contrast, uses a series of smaller, more modest experiments incorporated into public opinion surveys conducted by media organizations. By doing this, we trade some of the richer instrumentation available in omnibus surveys but gain some comparative advantages in return. Where other surveys are often tethered to an inflexible schedule, our approach makes us nimble. We can swoop in to areas of interest promptly, shining a spotlight on the thinking that underlies a particular conflict, even as it unfolds. And we can reflect on results—which hypotheses succeeded and which failed—and return to the field quickly to conduct follow-up experiments with refined hypotheses in hand.

We think this iterative approach is in the best tradition of scientific epistemology. It recognizes that, when it comes to science, the only sources of new insight are tentative, loosely formed intuitions, inspired by past experiences and wrong at least as often as they are right. As the great philosopher of science Karl Popper put it, "We do not know: we can only guess. . . . [W]e might describe our own contemporary science . . . as consisting of 'anticipations, rash and premature'" (Popper [1959] 2010, 278). Iterative experimentation allows us to test many premature anticipations with the benefit of reflection that can come only after an initial test. Further, iterative experimentation impels the researcher to present and reflect on failed tests and null results, also a valuable and often-neglected exercise (Ioannidis 2005). New ways to conduct randomized experiments inexpensively appear to be arising more and more frequently, so we mean to call attention to the value of this iterative approach.

In some cases, the iterative way in which we carried out our experiments requires an additional assumption. When we compare the results from one experiment to a separate experiment conducted at a different time, any differences that arise could come from the different nature of the experiments (as will generally be our interest), or they could arise from the intervention of time, such as if people began to think differently about racial profiling between time A and time B. We generally feel comfortable making this assumption for two reasons. First, the intervening time is small, generally a few weeks to a few months. Second, we monitored the news and other relevant factors for developments that could tinge the results of our studies, but found none.

We are almost ready to begin. Before we do, we should perhaps say something about our own perspectives. The issues we investigate in the pages that follow are thorny and complex. Experts and citizens alike contend over them precisely because there are no easy or obvious answers. It is not our intention to suggest otherwise. We hesitate, for instance, to characterize specific policies as "racially egalitarian" or even "advancing blacks' interests" because we recognize there is a meaningful debate—even among blacks—about whether these characterizations are apt. (We occasionally use terms like these for the sake of clarity, because to do otherwise would be cumbersome.) We also want to avoid being too grandiose in claiming that our "remedies" solve every problem. We note that *remedy* is commonly defined as a treatment, something that alleviates a problem, even if only partially and without removing the underlying cause. That said, we think that the ideas and evidence we marshal in these pages cast new light on the underpinnings of opinions and suggest ways that change—positive change—is possible.

CHAPTER 2

Ballot Architecture and the Building of Schools

Heresthetic, according to William Riker (1986), is the art of strategically structuring voting processes in order to manipulate outcomes. As he writes, "Winners induce by more than rhetorical attractions. Typically they win because they have set up the situation in such a way that other people will want to join them—or will feel forced by circumstances to join them—even without any persuasion at all. And this is what heresthetic is about: structuring the world so you can win" (p. ix).

It is not difficult to come up with real-world examples of heresthetical maneuvering. When the House of Representatives Rules Committee devises a "King of the Hill" rule that packages related bills together and offers them in a particular sequence, it is engaging in heresthetic. The rule stipulates that the last bill in the sequence to pass supersedes all of the previous bills, even if they too have passed. This rule thus has the ability to promote compromise by allowing representatives to vote for a pure "early" version of the bill (and tout that support back home in the district) as well as a (later) version that been politically negotiated (Smith, Roberts, and Vander Wielen 2006, 103). To offer another example, members of Congress find it politically unpalatable to raise their own salaries. Congress thus has established a commission that annually recommends pay raises for high-level members of the government. Congressional rules stipulate that the commission's recommendations go into effect unless Congress explicitly votes the recommendations down. If nobody chooses to bring it up, members need not vote to raise their own salaries. This mechanism thus makes a salary increase a much more likely outcome.[1]

What is striking about the political science literature on heresthetic is that it is centered on legislatures and does not extend to mass elections, which are not so easily manipulated, in part because the rules are so much less fluid. But the basic logic of heresthetic should apply to mass voting. Political scientists have shown, for instance, that the form that a ballot takes can influence how votes are cast. Such things as the order in which candidates appear on a ballot (Taebel 1975; Miller and Krosnick 1998), the ability to vote the party line with a single mark (Hamilton and Ladd 1996), and whether a ballot is organized by party column or office blocks (Walker 1966) can affect how people vote. Even something as simple as whether candidates are lined up in one column or two, as some Florida officials learned after the 2000 election, can affect outcomes, if only by accident.

The findings about ballot form are qualified, however. Ballot form appears to have its biggest impact among those least politically anchored and most easily manipulated, and its effect is most pronounced in low-information situations where the usual cues, like party identification and incumbency, are unavailable: nonpartisan elections, party primaries, open-seat elections, multimember legislative elections, and races at the bottom of the ballot. As Joanne M. Miller and Jon Krosnick (1998) summarize their findings, "All of this suggests that [ballot] structure influences election outcomes when voters lack substantive bases for candidate preferences" (p. 291; see also Mueller 1969; Darcy 1986). These findings do not make the best case for heresthetic. If heresthetic really makes a difference in electoral situations, the standards should be higher. A heresthetical electoral device should be purposeful, it should affect the decisions of voters who have preconceived ideas, even strong ideas, and it should influence by more than whim or accident.

In this chapter, we present a tough test of heresthetic in the electoral arena: a vote linked to race. In voting situations that involve racial issues, with prejudice, personal feelings, and ideological principle in the mix, it seems that a heresthetical device faces a special challenge. Moreover, electoral issues involving race often pit one group's interests against another's. Where this is the case, where blacks and other minorities constitute larger proportions of the population and racial competition evokes intergroup hostility, the attitudes involved are often especially hardened, particularly the attitudes of the more threatened group (Bobo 1999). Can a heresthetical device, a mere shaping of electoral choices on a ballot, help counter white hostility to black interests, even where blacks are a political force?

Our argument in this chapter is that indeed it can, that heresthetical maneuvering can lead whites to vote differently, even on an issue of race where black and white interests come into conflict. The inspiration for this argument is a real-world heresthetic experiment conducted in Jackson, Mississippi, in 1991: a creative "checklist" ballot that seemed to work, inasmuch as one can tell from electoral results. As we will discuss, the Jackson experiment is intriguing, but it raises as many questions as it answers. These questions set up this analysis, which we approach with our public opinion experiments. In a first set of experiments, we attempt to replicate the logic of Jackson's heresthetic to see if it is successful in changing votes (and white votes at that) in a group conflict situation. It is. In the second part of this chapter, we present two theoretical explanations derived from Riker's original work as to why heresthetic is effective. We then pit these two explanations against each other in a second set of experiments built on the first. The major finding is that the checklist device restructures and reframes the choice presented to voters and offers voters more psychological control over how resources are to be spent. The lessons—about disaggregation, control, and choice—have the potential to apply to other political issues that involve the distribution of resources to different competing groups.

An Unusual Election

The Jackson project was an attempt to pass school bonds, an election that required a large number of white voters to support schools that were (and continue to be) heavily black. Jackson was a 56 percent black city at that time, but blacks comprised 78 percent of students in the school district (1990 Census; Mississippi Department of Education 1999). Like many allocational issues at the local level, school finance elections often become captive to "community conflict" and the inability of the public "to [think] about the schools in other than racial terms" (Cataldo and Holm 1983, 629; see also Giles, Gatlin, and Cataldo 1976; Sharp 1987). The "only real hope," according to Everett F. Cataldo and John D. Holm (1983, 629), "would appear to be in attempting to break the connection between community conflict and school funding." This was the goal in Jackson.

In June 1991, voters in the city confronted a choice about their schools. On the ballot was a $74.9 million school bond issue. It had been some time since a bond issue had fared well in Jackson. Indeed, the last time a school bond issue passed in the city was 1964, back when Mississippi was the only state in the nation that had not even started to integrate its schools. That year, with a federal judge requiring several Mississippi counties to begin desegregation, the state legislature met in a special session called by the governor to provide an "escape hatch" for white parents who planned to remove their children from the newly desegregated schools (*New York Times* 1964). With new grants available to help pay for private, nonsectarian schools, white students began to leave the public schools en masse.

Even before 1964, school bond issues in Mississippi faced a very high barrier as the state legislature, in 1950, had passed a 60 percent rule. Under the rule, school bond issues could not pass in any district in the state without a 60 percent approval rate. In the civil rights and post–civil rights era, this was a threshold school officials in Jackson were unable to meet. The last attempt in Jackson had been in 1983, when the city failed, twice, to pass a bond issue.[2] In both elections, the bond issues fell well short with only 52 percent support.[3] Dr. Ben Canada, the city's school superintendent in 1991, recalls, "When I [came] to Jackson, I was told that [school bonds] didn't have a prayer. They said, 'Don't even ask for it.'"

But in 1991, school officials sponsoring the bond issue thought that they might just have a chance. They had a clever idea to restructure the ballot, an idea that was, according to Canada, an attempt to take advantage of voter psychology. First, he and the School Committee identified the ten most important infrastructure needs in the district. With that in hand, they put together a bond issue that was actually a set of ten "mini" bond issues, a checklist of different items that voters could choose to individually support or reject. Voters were able to cast separate votes to air-condition and renovate the schools, replace portable classrooms, purchase new library books, construct new science labs, purchase new computer equipment, and build new athletic facilities (see Table 2.1 for the complete list). With this novel approach to the ballot, a list of projects spread throughout the city, and a clear presentation of the needs of the school district, Canada lined up support from civic leaders, the *Jackson Clarion-Ledger*, the business community, and even administrators from some of Jackson's private academies in his quest for the elusive 60 percent. There was some disorganized opposition to the bond issue—an informal white supremacist network mobilized (Hayden 1991)—and there were those who can always be counted upon to vote no, but the pro forces were optimistic nonetheless.

Table 2.1. Results from 1991 Jackson School Bond Vote

	Cost of item (millions of dollars)	Vote to support (%)
Air-conditioning and renovations	29.6	63.24[a]
Replace portable classrooms	4.3	60.47[a]
Build and equip new classrooms	10.0	59.56
New library books	1.3	62.08[a]
New computer equipment	13.3	58.11
Build and equip new science labs	12.0	59.63
Improve school security	.7	58.33
Build athletic complex	3.0	49.02
Improve soccer fields	.6	49.61
Improve football fields and facilities	.1	51.47

[a] Passed given Mississippi state requirement of 60 percent support

The election was a nail-biter. Seven of the ten items on the list received support from between 58 and 63 percent, with five of them exceeding 60 percent after the votes were counted on election day. As the city clerk added absentee votes to the totals, however, two of the items on the list (science labs and new classrooms) fell just below 60 percent, and proponents were left with just three projects passing (Table 2.1). Though disappointed, they considered passage of the three items a victory, given the recent failures of these efforts and that voters approved about half the funding requested, including the most expensive item on the list—funding to air-condition and renovate all the schools in the district.

The election was an interesting exercise in political creativity. But it is unclear from looking at the results whether the checklist ballot really made a difference. There is, in fact, an alternative explanation for the 1991 success. Since 1983, the last time school bonds had been on the ballot, public attitudes toward education had evolved. While it is not possible to gauge what Jacksonians were thinking about education over this time, national attitudes toward education certainly changed in such a way as to encourage financial support for schools. Looking at over-time survey data from American National Election Studies and Gallup Polls shows this clearly (Table 2.2). In identifying the most important problems facing the country, an increasing number of respondents pointed to education in the years between 1984 and 1992 (from 2 percent in the former to 8 percent in the latter). Moreover, in the late 1980s and early 1990s, Gallup Polls found that Americans increasingly

Table 2.2. Concern for Education and Education Funding Is Heightened in the Early 1990s

	1984	1985	1986	1987	1988	1989	1990	1991	1992	1993	1994
Education most important problem (ANES)	2% (2,257)		5% (2,176)		6% (2,040)		7% (2,000)		8% (1,206)		9% (1795)
Perception of direction of local public schools											
Improved					29%		22%				26%
Gotten worse					19		30				37
Same					37		36				33
Don't know					15		12				4
					(2,118)		(1,594)				(1,326)
Public funding biggest problem faced by public schools (Gallup Poll)	14% (1,515)	9% (1,528)	11% (1,552)	14% (1,572)	12% (2,118)	13% (1,584)	13% (1,594)	18% (1,500)	22% (1,306)	21% (1,306)	13% (1,326)

Note: Number in parentheses is size of poll.

Question wording:

Education most important problem (American National Election Studies): "What do you think are the most important problems facing this country?" Up to three responses are coded. Percentage includes mention of education as any of the three problems identified by respondents. Although this question has been asked continually through the ANES series, the question wording periodically has changed. The wording did not change between 1984 and 1992.

Perception of direction of local public schools (Gallup Poll): "Would you say that the public schools in this/your community have improved from, say, five years ago, gotten worse, or stayed about the same?" The data come from the Annual Gallup Poll of the Public's Attitudes Toward the Public Schools, 1984–1994 and are reported annually in Phi Delta Kappan. The question wording changed modestly (*this* to *your*) in the 1994 survey.

Public funding biggest problem faced by public schools (Gallup Poll): "What do you think are the biggest problems with which the public schools in this community must deal?" Percentage is number of people mentioning "lack of proper financial support." The data come from the Annual Gallup Poll.

perceived local public schools as heading in the wrong direction. By 1994, almost twice as many people than in 1988 said that the schools had gotten worse. And respondents identified public funding as the biggest problem that public schools faced, with that sentiment reaching its peak in the early 1990s. Proponents of the 1991 bond issue also may simply have benefitted from a favorable public mood. James A. Stimson (1999, 123–125) argues that there was a liberal drift in public opinion in the late 1980s, perhaps in reaction to years of Reagan-Bush policies that climaxed in the early 1990s. There is no reason this should have happened everywhere but Mississippi. Simply looking at the results of the election and comparing them to the results from eight years prior thus does not allow for an evaluation of the effectiveness of the innovative ballot.

Nor do the simple election results allow one to approach other important questions. Did the checklist lead white voters to overcome their regular opposition to schools that mainly benefit black students? Without poll data or even some reasonable precinct-level aggregate data, it is hard to figure out how whites voted in the election. Moreover, voting behavior on school finance issues is influenced by many different factors—socioeconomic status, attitudes toward integration, and attitudes toward taxes in general, among other things (Giles, Gatlin, and Cataldo 1976; Hall and Piele 1976; Cataldo and Holm 1983; Sharp 1987)—and such things would need to be accounted for. If the checklist heresthetic did work, why did it work? Even if public opinion polls were available from Jackson in 1991, it is highly unlikely that the right questions would have been asked to understand what was behind the success of the checklist.

Checklist Versus Omnibus Responses

In this project, we roughly simulate the Jackson creative ballot with our set of public opinion experiments. The idea is not to replicate the situation perfectly—that is not possible—but to gain some insight on whether or not the ballot question does lead some individuals to think and behave differently, as well as to try to approach why it works (if in fact it does) and who responds to it most.

The sampling universe we use is not the city of Jackson but the entire state of Mississippi. One reason for this is that pollsters rarely confine their sample to a city of 193,000 like Jackson. By using a state-based survey, we also have access to people living in a variety of racial environments. The advantage of Mississippi, the most heavily black state in the nation, is the great variation in racial balance across the state. The fact that Mississippi counties range from having a black population of 4 percent (Tishomingo County) to 86 percent (Jefferson County) allows one to test whether the creative ballot works in different settings, even in those places where schools are overwhelmingly black. Moreover, with the exception of differences in racial balance, most Mississippi counties are generally comparable rural, small-town places.

Mason-Dixon Polling and Research conducted the two surveys containing our experiments. The surveys, both random-digit telephone surveys, took place in late September and early October 1999 and contained a battery of questions relating to Mississippi's November gubernatorial election. Given Mason-Dixon's purposes, the surveys only include individuals who were likely to vote in that election. This is not a problem for this study as these samples still offer a broad cross-section of people. Since our hypotheses relate to voting behavior, confining the experiments to likely voters even makes good sense.

To simulate the logic of the Jackson checklist ballot, we designed an experiment in which we offered a random half of survey respondents a question relating to their willingness to support a generic school bond. In that this question lumps together all the needs of the district, we label this the omnibus alternative: "As you may know, the schools in your district have many needs. Considering that it would lead to a modest increase in taxes, would you be willing to vote for a bond issue to improve and renovate schools in your district?" The other half of the respondents received a parallel question structured around their support of each of three items on a checklist:

> As you may know, the schools in your district have many needs. Considering that it would lead to a modest increase in taxes, would you be willing to vote for a bond issue to fund any or all of the following projects? Please tell me which projects you would be willing to fund:
> - A proposal to install or repair heating, air-conditioning, and plumbing systems in the schools.
> - A proposal to place more computers in classrooms.
> - A proposal to renovate locker rooms and gymnasiums.

These choices represent three of the items on the Jackson ballot, items that generated varying levels of support, one of them passing (the major infrastructure proposal), one failing but coming close to passage (computers), and one failing to even reach a simple majority (athletic facilities).

This is not, of course, a perfect simulation of the election that took place in Jackson. This only leads to a response to a question on a telephone survey that is divorced from a campaign and the considerations raised in a campaign. It does not have the potential to actually hit a voter's pocketbook in the same real and immediate way that a vote cast in an election would (though in both questions, we remind respondents that the bond issue would lead to an increase in taxes). And, unlike several of the proposals on the Jackson ballot, these checklist items are not tied to specific schools or facilities. Both versions of the question, however, are subject to these problems, and the goal is to compare the distribution of responses to the two forms of the question, which capture the basic logic of the omnibus and checklist ballots.[4]

The difference in responses to the two forms of the question is dramatic (Table 2.3). A fair majority of respondents in the omnibus treatment, about 56 percent of them, indicate that they would vote for a bond issue, but the number falls short of the 60 percent threshold required by Mississippi law. Two of the checklist items fare much better, with 68 percent of respondents indicating that they would vote to fund the heating/air-conditioning proposal and the computer proposal. Far fewer, 47 percent, would support the third proposal to renovate athletic facilities. While 68 percent of respondents approve of funding the first two items on the checklist, there is not complete overlap in support for these two items. A small number of people support heating and air-conditioning but not computers, and vice versa. Taking this into account, 74 percent of respondents in the second treatment indicate that they would support at least one of the items on the checklist, and 61 percent of respondents indicate that they would support at least two.[5] Comparing respondents supporting the omnibus issue with those supporting at least one checklist item, the checklist clearly has a significant effect on voter support.[6] Even comparing omnibus supporters with supporters of two of the items on the checklist (not shown in the table) yields an effect not that far from statistical significance ($p < 0.18$).

The checklist works, but does it work equally well for whites and blacks? This question is central to this enterprise, for our general purpose is to identify ways that whites can be led to support an allocation of resources that benefits

Table 2.3. Checklist Ballots Do Influence Mississippi Voters (Experiment 1)

	Omnibus (mean score)	Checklist (mean score)	Support for specific items		
			Heat, etc.	Computers	Gymnasiums, etc.
All	.56	.74	.68	.68	.47
	(387)	(393)	(370)	(372)	(353)
t	—	5.26***			
Whites	.45	.67	.61	.60	.29
	(288)	(274)	(225)	(259)	(245)
t	—	5.28***			
Blacks	.87	.89	.85	.87	.79
	(97)	(118)	(114)	(112)	(107)
t	—	.53			
		* $p < .10$	** $p < .05$	*** $p < .01$	

Source: Mason-Dixon Polling Sample and Research, Inc.

Notes: Sample is likely voters in Mississippi. Experiment was in the field for two consecutive days in late September 1999. Responses to all questions are coded 0 for "no," 1 for "yes." "Don't know" responses are coded as missing data. The checklist mean score is coded 1 if the respondent answered "yes" to any of the three items on the checklist, 0 if the respondent responded "no" and/or "don't know" to all three of the items on the checklist. To make the questions comparable, respondents who responded "don't know" to all three items on the checklist are classified as missing data on the checklist.

Question wording:

Omnibus question: As you may know, the schools in your district have many needs. Considering that it would lead to a modest increase in taxes, would you be willing to vote for a bond issue to improve and renovate schools in your district?

Checklist question: As you may know the schools in your district have many needs. Considering that it would lead to a modest increase in taxes, would you be willing to vote for a bond issue to fund any or all of the following projects? Please tell me which projects you would be willing to fund:

A proposal to install or repair heating, air-conditioning, and plumbing systems in the schools.

A proposal to place more computers in classrooms.

A proposal to renovate locker rooms and gymnasiums.

blacks. The Jackson election does not offer insight into this question, but we can approach the question by looking at the experimental findings by race.

The results are, at first glance, surprising. The experimental manipulation affects whites' responses much more dramatically than blacks'. Whites are much more likely to approve at least one item (and even two items) on the checklist than in the omnibus treatment. Whites are also very sensitive to the items being offered on the checklist, with huge variation in support for the various proposals. Over 60 percent of whites approve of school infrastructure improvements and additional computers, but only 29 percent approve of improvements to athletic facilities. For blacks, there is not much difference between support for the checklist and support for the omnibus plan. What small difference there is does not come close to achieving statistical significance. Moreover, there is only modest variation in support for the checklist proposals, with blacks slightly more likely to support the first two items than the athletic improvements. The explanation, of course, is a ceiling effect and, in this light, the results are perhaps less surprising. Blacks are so very highly supportive of an omnibus bond issue that it would be difficult for any other plan to generate increased support.

Uneven Success?

Does the heresthetic work with all whites in the same way? That is, do whites in heavily white places respond to the creative ballot much more than whites in heavily black places? If the checklist encourages whites to be more generous to schools mostly serving whites, but not to those mostly serving blacks, this is still an interesting device that school districts would be wise to look at. It would not contribute to overcoming racial hostility generated by group competition, however, and that is our ultimate focus.

To test how whites from different racial environments respond to the ballot innovation, we break the sample into three groups, with break points set by the proportion of black students in public schools. What is interesting about Mississippi, and consistent with a group conflict interpretation of political behavior (Bobo, Kluegel, and Smith 1997), is that the "blackness" of school districts is exaggerated by choices made by whites in heavily black places. As Figure 2.1 shows, as blacks become a larger proportion of those living within a school district, the schools within that district become even more racially skewed.[7] A school district that is 10 percent black is likely to have schools that are 10 percent black. At about 15 percent, the two numbers start to diverge, and school districts tend to be about 22 percent black. White abandonment of public schools accelerates as a district's population becomes more heavily black. The schools in Mississippi become majority black when the district is between 30 and 35 percent black. To capture basic differ-

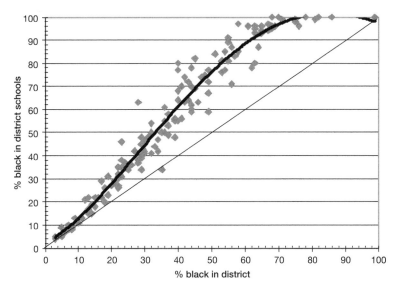

Figure 2.1. Racial Balance in Mississippi Schools, 1990s
Source: Mississippi Department of Education

ences between whites, we divide whites into those who live in counties that are less than 15 percent black, those who live in 16–35 percent black counties, and those who live in counties that are more than 35 percent black (we divide whites by county residence and not by school district as this is how Mason-Dixon collects residential information).

Results of the breakdown are in Table 2.4; the findings suggest two things. First, consistent with expectations derived from group conflict theory, it is clear from these results that group competition is contributing to white hostility toward black interests. Where blacks are a larger proportion of a population—and, more important, are direct beneficiaries of public money—whites are less likely to support the allocation of money to public schools. In almost every case, whites in more heavily black counties are less likely to support the bond issue, omnibus or checklist, than those in less black counties.[8] Only on the omnibus vote does the pattern break a bit. Yet even here, whites in the least black counties are most likely to vote for the bond issue.

While this relationship holds in these experiments, the checklist electoral device appears to improve white support for public schools about the same amount in less black and heavily black areas of Mississippi. On both experiments, the checklist contributes between 16 and 26 points to the mean

Table 2.4. Checklist Works for Whites in Various Racial Environments (Experiment 1)

	Omnibus (mean score)	Checklist (mean score)	Support for specific items		
			Heat, etc.	Computers	Gymnasiums, etc.
Percent black in county					
0–15%	.53	.76	.77	.66	.40
	(40)	(53)	(47)	(50)	(50)
t	—	2.35**			
16–35%	.43	.69	.62	.65	.32
	(151)	(105)	(95)	(99)	(93)
t	—	4.14***			
≥36%	.45	.61	.54	.52	.29
	(97)	(116)	(113)	(110)	(102)
t	—	2.33**			
		* p < .10	** p < .05	*** p < .01	

Note: See Table 2.3 for review of coding and analysis details.

score (the difference between the percentage of whites supporting the omnibus bond and the percentage of whites supporting at least one item on the checklist). It does not even out the differences between whites in heavily black and less black areas but it does not expand those differences, either. If this were just a matter of leading whites to support their own interests, that expansion would have occurred. Most important, the checklist draws more than enough white support. Combining substantial white support with overwhelming black support, the checklist appears to generate a comfortable victory for the schools, even in the most heavily black parts of the state.

Theoretical Explanations for Success

These results, while they do not perfectly replicate the Jackson election, do suggest that this political device has great potential, if not to pull large numbers of people (whites) over the line of support for each and every item, then to make it possible to win on at least some issues that might otherwise have failed. Why was this particular heresthetic effective? How did it persuade some white voters to support the schools? Riker's work suggests two different alternative explanations. First, he argues that the success of many heresthetical devices lies with the manipulation of dimensions voters rely upon in making decisions. In many cases, this means that the heresthetician simply reframes the issue, adding dimensionality by introducing new considerations to the decision. As voters are encouraged to reevaluate their own proximity to the existing alternatives on more than the count or counts that had mattered before, and to apply previously untapped attitudes to the decision, the choices they make may change.

In the case of the checklist, perhaps it is the specificity of the items on the list that raises new considerations for voters. By this line of logic, people are responding to new stimuli, and their approach to the question goes beyond the issue of how much they will be taxed and who will benefit from their tax money to the importance they place on the specific items being requested. Any specific item may have particular appeal to certain voters who otherwise might not be inclined to support a school bond issue. Those who value computer literacy, for example, will not be cued to think about this benefit in the omnibus treatment. And those who had not previously thought about how hot it must be in the schools in June might look at the tax increase differently in the context of the checklist. This is consistent with recent work by William Jacoby (2000), who shows that specificity influences individual attitudes toward government spending and does so dramatically. In his analysis, large numbers of individuals generally opposed to government spending ease their hostility to it when it is framed in specific terms (identifying the actual targets of the spending, as well as the reasons why the spending is important). The different choices people make, in this context, attest to the power of the specific frame.

Perhaps even more important than the new considerations brought to the vote choice, the checklist may be working because it takes a consideration *out* of the equation that voters rely upon (what Riker refers to as "fixing dimensionality"). An often-used reason for hostility to local and state taxes is that the tax revenues go to support bloated bureaucracies and never make it to the ultimate destination (Sears and Citrin 1982, 50–53).[9] Designating the money for very specific projects (and infrastructure projects at that) removes any question as to where the money would be going. While waste and bureaucracy may still be on some people's minds when they cast their votes on the checklist items, there is far less left to the imagination and less chance that voters will think about bureaucrats (or hear opponents of the measure talk about bureaucratic waste) when approaching this decision.

A second explanation for the success of heresthetical devices is that they change the structure of the choice, sometimes simply offering new choices, other times altering the way or order in which issues will be considered. Riker calls this "agenda control," and the key is simply to change voting rules or procedures in such a way as to favor one position over another. Clearly, this is at work with the checklist. In part, the checklist procedure offers voters ten choices instead of one, giving them many intermediate positions between "all" and "nothing" to help the schools. Even if these intermediate positions pull voters away from the all and the nothing positions equally, the schools will gain since they benefit more from the diminution in outright opposition than they lose from the diminution of complete support. In part, it simply may be that the items on the checklist by themselves will take less from the taxpayer than the omnibus proposal. This explanation seems a bit less likely, given that research shows that voters tend to be insensitive to the cost of ballot measures.[10] So argues Donald P. Green (1992, 139) in his analysis of the price elasticity of public goods. Instead of cost, he writes, it is "the potency of negative symbols such as bureaucratic waste, big government, and undeserving beneficiaries [that] often determines the fate of tax-related ballot measures."

It is more than the number of choices to be made or the fact that the question posed to voters changes from "Should I support the bond issue?" to "What should I support in the bond issue?" that makes the restructuring of the choice powerful. Respondents also may be reacting favorably to the ability to control how their money is being allocated in the checklist situation. The argument here is not so much that the items on the list are somehow attractive to people, but rather that the restructured choices offer respondents/voters some role in deciding how their money is to be spent. It brings the average voter into the decision-making process, and this empowerment leads voters to be perhaps more generous than they otherwise might have been. As Superintendent Canada explains it, people want to say no to something: "We figured out the psychological piece, that you have to account for the fact that people won't vote for everything and this gives them a chance to do that. By giving people some say, we got this passed. I firmly believe that." In some sense, this argument is akin to the nonseparable preferences argument made by Dean Lacy (2001), who shows that various political decisions are interlinked and interdependent. By creating a situation whereby voters are able to vote against some items, it makes them more amenable to vote for others. This ability to vote both for and against the schools, we hypothesize, is empowering.

The added virtue of this alternative explanation is that it addresses one of the root causes of white reluctance to support institutions that predominantly serve African Americans. If white decisions about the allocation of resources among whites and blacks are informed by a view that black gains inevitably come at the expense of whites, it is not that surprising that we find, over and over, that whites are hostile to blacks. This political device offers something back to the white voter, that is, participation in the allocation process and perhaps some sense of control in it. It is not something tangible returned to whites as a group, but it does change the calculus a little, perhaps enough to change people's minds.

New Dimensions Versus Reconstructed Choices

In a second set of experiments built on the first, we pit these two explanations—the introduction of new dimensions and the restructuring of the choice—against each other. This set of experiments was conducted in Mississippi in a second Mason-Dixon poll conducted just weeks after the first. There is no reason to believe that the small break between the two polls would lead to any changes in aggregate support for school bonds. In this case, the questions are constructed differently to test the power of the two explanations.

In the second experiment, the omnibus question is offered in the same form except that the three projects are detailed in the question. Respondents are thus offered specificity—they will know where their tax money is or is not going—but not disaggregation or control. The checklist question also is modified in the second experiment. Respondents are presented with a more general checklist with items phrased to give voters less detail on how their tax money is to be spent, thus offering disaggregated choices and voter control but not much specificity (see Table 2.5 for question wordings).[11] If the key to the success of the checklist items is the new dimension introduced into the choice—that is, considerations raised by more precise knowledge of the needs of the district—then the specific omnibus question should generate more support for the school bond than the general omnibus question and the difference between the specific omnibus and the general checklist

Table 2.5. Disaggregation and Specificity in Checklist Responses (Experiment 2)

	Specific omnibus (mean score)	General checklist (mean score)	Support for specific items		
			Infrastructure	Technology	Athletic facilities
All	.60	.77	.71	.72	.51
	(300)	(285)	(264)	(272)	(254)
t	—	4.62***			
Whites	.50	.70	.65	.64	.36
	(220)	(198)	(181)	(189)	(173)
t	—	4.07***			
Blacks	.85	.94	.83	.92	.82
	(78)	(87)	(83)	(83)	(81)
t	—	2.05**			

Whites Only

	Specific omnibus (mean score)	General checklist (mean score)	Support for specific items		
			Infrastructure	Technology	Athletic facilities
Percent black in county					
0–15%	.64	.81	.79	.74	.48
	(36)	(32)	(29)	(31)	(29)
t	—	1.6			

16–35%	.51	.71	.64	.63	.37
	(113)	(84)	(75)	(78)	(71)
t	—	2.89***			
≥36%	.42	.63	.61	.60	.32
	(71)	(82)	(77)	(80)	(73)
t	—	2.66**			

* $p < .10$ ** $p < .05$ *** $p < .01$

Source: Mason-Dixon Polling Sample and Research, Inc. Sample is likely voters in Mississippi. The survey was in the field for two consecutive days in October 1999. See Table 2-3 for review of coding and analysis details.

Question wording:

<u>Specific omnibus question</u>: As you may know, the schools in your district have many needs. Considering that it would lead to a modest increase in taxes, would you be willing to vote for a bond issue that would allow your school district to install or repair heating, air-conditioning, and plumbing systems in the schools, to place more computers in the classrooms, and to renovate locker rooms and gymnasiums?

<u>General checklist question</u>: As you may know the schools in your district have many needs. Considering that it would lead to a modest increase in taxes, would you be willing to vote for a bond issue to fund any or all of the following projects? Please tell me which projects you would be willing to fund:

A proposal to improve and repair school buildings.
A proposal to improve technology in the schools.
A proposal to improve athletic facilities.

treatment should diminish greatly. If it is the structure of the ballot, the disaggregation of choices, and the sense of participation in the allocation process that matters, the general checklist should continue to perform well vis-à-vis the omnibus treatment and the difference between the omnibus and checklist treatments should persist.

Results from the second set of experiments show that specificity does not explain much of the success of the checklist. Identifying the specific projects to be funded by the omnibus bond issue does improve support for the bond issue and support does reach the magic 60 percent threshold, but the improvement is small (Table 2.5). Somewhat surprisingly, the general checklist also generates improved support, respondents finding the more general alternatives a bit more attractive than the more specific versions, on each of the items as well as on the overall score. Breaking the results down by race shows essentially the same patterns as before. The only difference is that in this second experiment, blacks offer greater support for checklist items than the omnibus item, mostly because of the very high support for the technology proposal. That aside, the results of the second experiment look much like the results from the first experiment. The checklist, even with general information, evokes more support for the schools than the omnibus treatment that specifically identifies where the money is to go.

To summarize, while both the introduction of a new dimension into the choice and the restructuring of the choice appear to contribute to the success of this creative ballot, it is the latter that provides the crucial difference. First, it gives voters more precision in expressing their preference and inevitably leads many away from outright opposition. This comes at the cost of losing some who completely supported the schools in the all-or-nothing case, but that is a trade-off well worth making. Arthur Lupia and Richard Johnston (2001) make the case that voters would be more competent if elites offered more than a binary choice on referenda. But in most cases, they argue, the logistics of giving many choices instead of two are impossible, and they look elsewhere for improving competence. This checklist does feasibly offer voters more choices and, without much added complexity, increases voter competence, with benefits for the schools.

In changing the structure of the choice in this particular way, voters also are offered some semblance of control in the process. It is not a tangible economic benefit but a political benefit that whites receive, and in giving whites this semblance of control, there is the potential to change minds. As Paul M. Sniderman and Thomas Piazza (1993, 165) argue, on many racial issues, large numbers of whites are persuadable. "New majorities can be made and un-made," they write, "the future is not foreordained. It is the business of poli-tics to decide it."

An Optimistic Conclusion

School boards and local officials are often masters of heresthetic and go to great lengths to improve the electoral prospects of school bonds. Officials of-ten schedule school finance elections apart from general elections to depress turnout and to raise opponents' cost of voting. They schedule short lead times to the election to keep the opposition from coalescing. They avoid tax days, summer vacation, and the Christmas holidays because these times clearly limit who is likely to show up to the polls. And they prefer elections during the school year when needs can be better articulated and parent volunteers can be more easily organized (Dunne, Reed, and Wilbanks 1997). All these strategies are directed to issues of mobilization and turnout, attempts to achieve a favor-able supporter/opponent ratio. In Jackson, school officials did this, scheduling a special election in June, when school was still in session and the need for air-conditioning could not be more apparent. But they also attempted to do something more ambitious. They tried to influence the decisions of voters.

Our results show that they very likely were successful. The questions posed to respondents in these experiments do not perfectly simulate a ballot and do not get at questions of mobilization. But they do suggest, in support of the results in the Jackson election, that heresthetical maneuvering is pos-sible on school bond referenda (and possibly on other kinds of referenda as well). These results should encourage those seeking to run effective cam-paigns on behalf of schools, campaigns that take place all over the country every year. These experiments go beyond this, however. They show that ra-cial hostility—at least some of the racial hostility generated by competition over the allocation of resources—can be overcome somewhat, even in the South, even in Mississippi. Progress can be made via politics and how poli-tics is practiced.

CHAPTER 3

Following Neighbors, If Not Leaders

In 1962, during the centennial of the Civil War, South Carolina's state legislature passed a bill to raise the Confederate flag atop the state capitol in Columbia. They did not indicate when it should come down. Whether as an act of white defiance during the civil rights movement or a simple oversight, the flag was not removed from the dome at the end of the centennial celebration. As time passed, many whites came to view the capitol flag as a symbol of heritage and ancestral pride in this, the most "southern" of all the southern states (Reed 1972, p. 18). Blacks almost uniformly saw it as a symbol of enslavement and oppression. Because this particular version of the flag had been adopted by the Ku Klux Klan in the 1930s, its meaning was particularly tainted, equivalent to a swastika for many.

As African Americans began to more assertively press their political interests, the racial controversy grew to ever-larger proportions. Several attempts to forge compromise between the two hard-line positions failed in the 1980s and 1990s, so that in 2000, when Governor Jim Hodges attempted to revive the effort, there was widespread skepticism. Ultimately, Hodges and members of the state legislature, both white and black, forged a multi-faceted compromise in a prolonged political drama. The story is a fascinating one, and the process in South Carolina offers a wonderful opportunity to study how members of the mass public, particularly whites being asked to relinquish something valued, respond to real world politics.

Policymaking is inevitably an exercise in compromise. Success depends upon balancing multiple interests even if the final product most often fails to meet the complete satisfaction of those who agree to it. The political process, in all its different dimensions, is essentially a quest for the acceptable if not the ideal. In this chapter, we look at how members of the mass public respond to political processes, particularly political negotiation and successful compromise, and seek to understand what it is about such compromise that people might respond to. We are especially interested in whether political compromise on a racial issue can elicit a positive public response, especially important given how divisive such issues can be and how resistant they can be to resolution.

Political scientists recently have begun to pay attention to how regular citizens respond to the workings of politics. John Hibbing and Elizabeth Theiss-Morse (2001) argue that Americans respond less to policy outputs and more to policy inputs, and that "attitudes toward the *processes* of government, as apart from the *policies*, constitute an important, free-standing variable that has serious implications for the health of democracy" (147, emphasis in original). Not surprisingly, much of the public response to process is negative. Given how messy, prolonged, and combative politics can be, it makes sense that the public would find distasteful the little they see of it. As Hibbing and Theiss-Morse argue, public dissatisfaction with Congress flows from its "open and bruising process" (147), as well as interest group participation, partisan squabbling, legislative delay and political manipulation. Along these lines, Robert Durr and colleagues (1997, 176) argue that "the very activities which characterize Congress and the legislative process—deliberation, debate, and decision making—cause it to appear quarrelsome, unproductive, and controversial, and thus diminish it in the public eye."

What of successful politics and political compromise? Given that principle is highly valued by people, even the compromise required by representative democracy can become unattractive. Within a legislature, the ability to broker agreements, find commonality, and accommodate differences is valued—one is reminded of the words of Minority Leader Everett Dirksen, "I'm a man of principle, and one of my principles is flexibility"—but this ability does not appear to be wholly valued outside the institution. Some, mostly ideologues, undoubtedly prefer no loaf to half of one. Durr and colleagues (1997, 182) also argue, in the context of Congress, that because our political process is open and because Congress's activities are generally well covered, policy disagreements are aired. "When the bargaining and amending are done," they speculate, "the finished product appears not as a coherent whole, but as a patchwork of compromises, each of which was controversial and to some extent alienating." They write that overall, "Congress is unpopular for being itself," a point supported by the fact that periods of greater levels of legislative activity and output also tend to be periods of lower levels of congressional popularity.

If there are suggestions that political compromise is a turnoff, there are also reasons to believe that people respond favorably to it. For a problem that has been festering for a long time, political compromise represents resolution, or at least the promise of it. For a prolonged stalemate, especially one that crowds out other problems or other news items, issue fatigue may lead some individuals to welcome a compromise that makes the debate go away.

On an issue where a political compromise helps diminish high-profile group differences, perhaps the simple fact of compromise has some ameliorative influence on members of the groups involved. Our group conflict theoretical perspective suggests that political processes should necessarily heighten group competition and that members of the mass public should respond to this competition if they know about it. But what happens when politics resolves competition?

Compromise and legislative success also require majority rule. If a compromise position is perceived to represent majority will in the general public, one also might expect the compromise to win support beyond those who actually approve of the solution. There is a certain residual respect for majority rule and the stamp of legitimacy that comes with passage of a law. Sniderman and Piazza (1993, 132), for instance, show that support for minority set-asides grows when respondents are told that Congress has passed laws to ensure them. A policy that is the final product of a real political process thus earns more favor than that very same policy posed as a hypothetical law. It also could be that some individuals may be more psychologically comfortable standing with the majority than outside it. Generating an impression of majority sentiment thus can lead to a snowballing effect, even among those who are not yet fully "on board" (Noelle-Neumann 1984). Finally, group conflict theory suggests that racial hostility stems from a majority-minority dynamic, with racial advantages justified by majority status and sentiment. What happens when this justification dissipates via political processes?

In the context of the Confederate flag controversy in South Carolina, we investigate whether people in the mass public reacted favorably or unfavorably to the political process that addressed the issue. We look at who was most likely to accept the compromise crafted through the political process. And we attempt to tease out what it is about political compromise that might bring some people to support the solution that comes from it—an empirical question, to be sure, but one rooted in our normative concerns about race relations and the role politics can play in improving them.

The Course of the Issue

The question of bringing down South Carolina's Confederate flag had received periodic attention from politicians since 1962, though it was only in the 1990s that the state's black leadership started to seriously strategize about how to change the situation.[1] By 1994, the state legislature (with an unprecedented number of seats being held by African Americans) took up the Heritage Act, a compromise to remove the flag from the dome and place it at the site of a Confederate memorial on the capitol grounds. While the proposal passed the state senate, the bill did not make it out of the house, largely because of opposition from Republican legislators. With Republican voters supporting the dome flag by a three-to-one margin on an "advisory" proposition vote on the 1994 primary ballot, who could blame them? Republican gubernatorial candidate David Beasley also took note of the predominant Republican sentiment on the issue and promised voters that he would support keeping the flag where it was.

After lying dormant for a couple of years, the proposal was revived by none other than Governor Beasley in late 1996. After a summer featuring some high-profile church burnings, and with the freedom that comes with political popularity, Beasley reversed his position on the flag and publicly called for it to come down. The governor's allies in the state legislature took up the issue when the legislature returned to work in early 1997, but opposition to Beasley's plan among Republican legislators was too vigorous, and even black Democrats showed little enthusiasm for the bill. While even Senator Strom Thurmond supported Beasley—as did all of the state's other living governors—the proposal died. In killing it, Republican state legislators called for a binding referendum to settle the issue, a proposal that was in part political cover, in part a prediction of the outcome. Indeed, the referendum became important to how flag proponents strategized against the proposal, "Majority Rule" being the slogan used by pro-flag groups and a serious theme in the rhetoric of pro-flag politicians (Heilprin 1997).

A referendum never materialized, and the most obvious outcome of the whole episode is that Governor Beasley became a vulnerable incumbent. Indeed, Beasley would later claim that black leaders and the NAACP cynically went AWOL during the episode in order to hurt him politically (*Charleston Post and Courier* 1999). Clearly it did. He was on record on the issue and on record supporting a proposal he had campaigned against that was unpopular with his core constituents. During his reelection campaign in 1998, flag proponents raised the issue—"Dump Beasley, Keep the Flag" was a frequent refrain—and Beasley's loss to Democratic candidate Jim Hodges was interpreted in the media to be partly due to his attempt to bring down the flag. Indeed, in the gubernatorial campaign, Hodges made no promises regarding the flag, though he made it clear that he personally favored its removal.

If Hodges dodged the issue in his campaign, it soon became apparent that he would not be able to avoid it upon becoming governor. The following July, the leaders of the South Carolina National Association for the Advancement of Colored People (NAACP) announced their intention to lead a tourism boycott of the state if the flag did not come off the capitol dome by the end of the year. With tourists spending $6.8 billion in the state in 1998 (Simmons 1999), and with the possibility of conventions and events pulling out of the state, the NAACP hoped to gain leverage that heretofore had been missing. At the request of the South Carolina chapter, the national NAACP joined the boycott, and as the year ended, numerous religious and political organizations, the National Collegiate Athletic Association (NCAA), and over seventy families had all relocated meetings, conventions, sporting events, and reunions to other states (M. Davis 1999). From within the state, the mayors of Charleston and Columbia, the football and basketball coaches of the state universities, and the Chamber of Commerce all sought to bring about resolution to the growing controversy.

Although Republican leaders and the most vigorous advocates of the flag chafed at the idea of acting in response to the boycott, several other highly symbolic initiatives moved forward in the closing months of 1999. With South Carolina the only state that did not have an official state holiday honoring Martin Luther King Jr., Governor Hodges proposed a King holiday in exchange for the end of the boycott. While the NAACP rejected his offer— "The short answer [is] no. The long answer [is] hell no," said a national NAACP leader (Strope 1999b)—legislation to create the holiday was filed in the state legislature. Additionally, a memorial to the state's black history won legislative approval for placement on the grounds of the capitol.[2]

As the New Year deadline passed, Governor Hodges announced that he was developing a plan to forge compromise and met privately with both flag proponents and flag opponents over several weeks in an attempt to put together a political solution that could pass the state legislature. By mid-February he was ready to move forward with his negotiated plan, a compromise based on previous attempts to bring the flag down, but with some new wrinkles. Hodges publicly proposed removing the Confederate Navy Jack from the capitol and placing a different flag, the square flag of the Confederate Army of Northern Virginia (one not tainted by association with the Ku Klux Klan) by a statue of a Confederate general at an obscure location on the capitol grounds. Hodges's plan, which also removed the flag from the house and senate chambers, yet preserved Confederate street names and other public monuments to Confederate war figures, was introduced in both the senate and the house by his legislative allies.

Over the next several months, the high-profile legislation slowly evolved.[3] Flag proponents in the legislature, after initially rejecting the compromise, came to accept it after some logrolling that massaged the symbolism of the change. Their support depended upon locating the flag at a more prominent memorial at a busy intersection in front of the statehouse and guaranteeing that the new placement could not be undone by a future legislative vote. Negotiations over the site of the flagpole (at the back of the memorial), the height of the flagpole (twenty feet), the security of the site (a new fence), and the nighttime display of the memorial (lights) slowly settled those issues. Ultimately, the delicate plan passed the state senate, and did so with six (of seven) black senators supporting the bill as well as Senator Glenn McConnell (the owner of a Confederate memorabilia shop) and several other leading flag advocates. The bill included the change to the Virginia flag and the removal of the flag from senate and house chambers. The more conservative house also passed the compromise, though the senate's proposal was modified on a couple of points (most notably raising the height of the flagpole to thirty feet). Not everyone accepted the compromises. Indeed, the NAACP, reacting to the senate plan, encouraged black representatives in the house to reject it on account of the new site, and all but three of the twenty-six voted no. Enough flag proponents voted in favor, however, for the bill to pass. Governor Hodges signed the bill in May, and the flag came down July 1. Said the governor in a televised speech, "Today, we bring this debate to an honorable end. Today, the descendants of slaves and the descendants of Confederate soldiers join together in the spirit of mutual respect. Today, the debate over the Confederate flag above the Capitol dome passes into South Carolina history" (Davenport 2000).

This was a long and messy process that started out at the beginning of the year in private negotiations and ended up being debated passionately until its passage. Most important, from our perspective, it was a process that large numbers of people cared about and easily understood, and it received an enormous amount of attention from both local and national media. In fact, at the end of 2000, Associated Press reporters voted the removal of the flag the "top South Carolina story of the year" (Baca 2000). If one were looking for an issue and a political process that the mass public was likely to respond to, this would be it.

The Public Response to the Confederate Compromise

Notably, the public response to the compromise generally appears to have been favorable. Inasmuch as one can tell, public support for compromise rose as the political process unfolded. Shortly after the NAACP announced its tourism boycott (in September 1999), one survey measured support for the compromise solution at 29 percent (Strope 1999a). By late December, as the governor, confronting the impending boycott, made it plain that he was working to resolve the issue with all sides represented, about 40 percent of South Carolinians supported a compromise solution (Associated Press 2000a). When the governor announced the contours of his plan after several intensive weeks of prelegislative negotiation, the split in the public was about fifty-fifty (49 percent for compromise; Associated Press 2000b). Over the next several months, support even grew modestly from there. Once the senate passed a version of the compromise in April (the house had yet to vote), one survey measured support for the compromise at 56 percent (Associated Press 2000c). These surveys were conducted by different organizations using different question wordings and different response categories, so it would be foolish to claim any precision in these comparisons. Nonetheless, tracing results across time offers some sense that public support for a compromise on the flag did build, with some relation to events taking place in the state capitol. This gave the politicians working on it some freedom to craft the compromise and resolve the immediate issue.

How do we know that people were actually responding to the political process and the compromise that emerged from it? At the time, one common speculation for public support for the compromise was that many South Carolinians had simply become weary of the controversy. "I think [support for the compromise] reflects flag fatigue," said Senator McConnell. "I think people are tired of hearing about it and are looking for a settlement." This was also the interpretation of the pollster: "[A lot of people] want [the flag] issue to go away" (Associated Press 2000b).

Flag fatigue is a plausible explanation for why many people would find compromise attractive and why that number might grow as the issue played out over many months. But it does not explain why support for the compromise would be low to start with. After all, the issue had been brewing for several years. People had ample time to tire of the controversy by the time the pollsters started asking about it in the fall of 1999.

Another possible explanation for the growth over time in support of the compromise is that people were responding to the NAACP boycott and its economic effects and not to the political process. The timing of events works better for this explanation than the flag fatigue explanation, with support for the compromise building after the intent to boycott was announced, and especially after the boycott went into effect. Business groups were alarmed by the boycott, and the state's newspapers reported that it was having a real, if not huge, economic impact on the tourism industry. The problem with this line of argument, however, is that the NAACP never offered to call off the boycott if the compromise was reached (and, indeed, the boycott operated throughout the decade). If people responded to the boycott and not the compromise, it was on an act of faith. This is not to say that the boycott was unimportant here. It clearly created the political pressure to settle the issue and it hovered over the process at every point. It seems less likely that people, black or white, were responding directly to it in coming to accept the compromise.

Not surprisingly, there is some indication that there was also a hostile reaction to the compromise from some quarters in the state. As one might predict, given a group conflict orientation, the challenge to the flag led many of those who held it most dear to hold it even closer. A couple of pieces of evidence suggest that this reaction was taking place simultaneously with the growth in support for the compromise. As it became possible that the flag might be coming down, the state experienced a huge surge in demand for "used" Confederate flags (those flown atop the state capitol). As shown in Figure 3.1, in the last months of fiscal year 2000, which coincided with the final months of the flag's stay atop the capitol, the state's used-flag sales boomed. While the state sold roughly 300–400 U.S. and South Carolina flags in 1999 and 2000, and about that many Confederate flags in 1999, it sold more than 17,000 Confederate flags in 2000. The demand even necessitated a capitol employee to continually run flags up and down the flagpole to

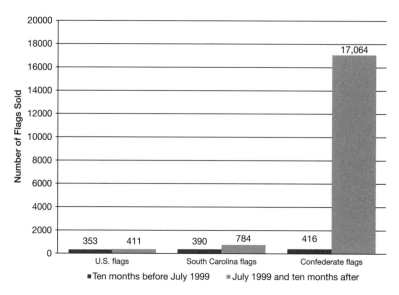

Figure 3.1. Flag Sales in South Carolina
Source: South Carolina Budget and Control Board

authentically use them. This privatization of the Confederate flag makes the growth in acceptance of the compromise even more remarkable.

Another hint of a very hostile reaction to the flag compromise is that there was a spate of racial violence in the state during the period of negotiations. Here, we must be a bit cautious, as hate crime data from the 1990s are not particularly reliable (and before 1996, they are unevenly available). Moreover, different states and localities defined and reported hate crimes differently, and standards likely changed over time. Still, looking at trends in hate crimes over time can make aberrant periods stand out. We do this for South Carolina in Figure 3.2, with similar time trends for nearby North Carolina and the United States as a whole shown for comparison.

Looking at the figure, it seems quite clear that South Carolina exhibited a notable spike in 1997 and 1998—precisely the years during which the compromise was being negotiated. The average annual number of hate crimes was nearly double the number of hate crimes reported in the state in the year before and the year after the political negotiations. The phenomenon does not appear to be a regional or national one, since hate crimes were actually decreasing in nearby North Carolina and the United States as a whole during the same period. What is going on is particular to South Caro-

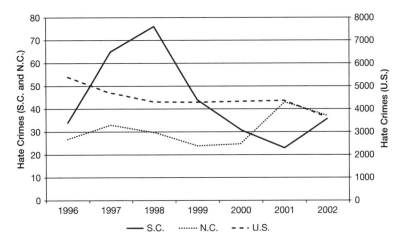

Figure 3.2. Racial Hate Crimes in South Carolina, North Carolina, and U.S.
Source: FBI Uniform Crime Reporting Program, *Hate Crime Statistics* (1996–2002)

lina. While this is indirect evidence and while the number of hate crimes is minuscule compared to all crimes committed in the state in this time, it nonetheless offers the possibility that the compromise evoked a powerful reaction from a tiny minority in the state.

Who Moves to Compromise?

Clearly not everyone is equally disposed to find political compromise acceptable. Certain kinds of people should be more likely than others to support compromise, and there is some practical value in knowing who these people are. Politicians, in particular, might find it useful to know where to turn for support after they craft a compromise, especially on a salient electoral issue like the flag. There is also some theoretical value to looking at the patterns of public support for compromise. A situation like this one offers an opportunity to explore general ideas about what encourages people to accept political compromise on racial issues. Here we test two hypotheses about who moves to compromise, both of them flowing from our group conflict theoretical understanding of racial-political attitudes.

If group competition has a distinct effect on racial-political attitudes, it follows that a diminishment of racial competition should allow people to soften their positions without changing their deep-seated feelings toward other groups. Our first hypothesis is thus that public support for the political compromise should come even from people with sentiments and beliefs about the flag, not just from those without an opinion.

Group conflict theory also suggests a second hypothesis. The political clash of groups should have a larger effect on those in the dominant group, on the group with something to lose instead of something to gain (Bobo 1999; Sidanius et al. 2000). Indeed, a focus on the attitudes of the dominant group is an element common to related theories such as racial threat theory, group position theory, and social dominance theory, and it is consistent with psychological theory that shows that individuals are much more likely to consider losses than gains as they assess a situation (Kahneman and Tversky 1984). In the Confederate flag situation, the theoretical expectation would thus be that whites supporting the flag should be more resistant to compromise than blacks seeking to bring the flag down. First, flag proponents face losing some state-sanctioned status, the type of symbolic loss that should engender a different perspective on the situation. Second, the compromise involves a move away from the status quo. Even if the compromise means only partial movement toward removing the flag, it still represents a gain for flag opponents. For flag proponents, the compromise can only be interpreted as a loss from their present position. Our expectation, then, is that support for the compromise should be asymmetrical, coming more from flag opponents than proponents.

The data we rely upon to test our two hypotheses come from two public opinion surveys conducted in South Carolina upon which we placed our question-wording experiments. The surveys, again conducted by the Mason-Dixon polling firm, were of registered voters in the weeks prior to the 2000 South Carolina Republican presidential primary. The first survey was in the field January 18–19, sampling registered likely voters about their views on various political issues in the state. The second survey went into the field a few weeks later on February 14–15. This survey was limited to Republican likely voters.[4] Given our interest in studying whites supportive of the Confederate flag and given that there is a much larger concentration of such people in a Republican sample, this second survey was of value to us.

In our experiments, we attempt to simulate the psychological process required by compromise. First we ask respondents their position on the flag controversy, with the question posed as a binary choice: take the flag down or leave it up. This provides us with a baseline of their original position. No matter what their answer, we then ask respondents a follow-up that offers three choices, the middle one being the compromise "to remove the Confederate battle flag from the statehouse dome, but move it to a monument or other place of honor on the statehouse grounds" (see Table 3.1 for exact question wording). The methodological advantage of posing the question in two stages is that the first question enables us to identify the direction that compromisers are coming from.

As noted in the previous section, levels of support for the compromise in January 2000 were fairly high. In the Mason-Dixon survey, just short of a majority of respondents accept the Confederate compromise. What is striking is that compromise supporters are both black and white (Table 3.1). Indeed, just about 50 percent of both races support the compromise, this despite the fact that they hold vastly different views of the flag. Over three-quarters of blacks (77 percent) in this survey agree with the argument that the Confederate flag is a symbol of racism. Only 9 percent take the position that it is a symbol of southern heritage. On the other hand, 66 percent of South Carolina whites view the flag as a symbol of heritage, while 21 percent equate it with racism.[5] Clearly, the compromise does not just generate support from those with no views on the subject (only 13–14 percent of the sample) but rather from those who, on principle, take one of the polar positions.

That there is significant (and almost equivalent) support for the compromise from both whites and blacks supports our first group conflict hypothesis but would seem to defy the second expectation of asymmetry. There is another way to test this expectation, however. The true test is not simply how many blacks and whites support the compromise, but whether the compromise alternative leads people to actually moderate their positions. Does support for the compromise come equally from white flag proponents and black flag opponents?

To approach this question, we set up an analysis confined to white flag proponents and black flag opponents (those who anchor themselves as such in the first question). We then regress whether or not people accept the compromise on the race variable. If there is a racial asymmetry to the movement to compromise, we should see it here. Additionally, we add controls for sex, age, and racial environment to the equation. Are women more likely to move to compromise than men? Are older people perhaps more set in their views? Does living in a heavily black county make people less likely to compromise? Since a more heavily black racial environment is likely to mean something different for blacks and for whites, we also include an interaction term. This

Table 3.1. Acceptance of the Confederate Flag Compromise

Remove Confederate flag? As you may know, some have called for the removal of
the Confederate flag flying over South Carolina's statehouse dome. Do you favor or
oppose removing the Confederate flag from over the statehouse?

	Whites (%)	Blacks (%)
Remove flag	39	86
Leave flag up	48	7
Don't know (volunteered)	13	7

Support flag compromise? Which of the following options would you prefer? To
remove the Confederate battle flag from the statehouse dome and not display it
anywhere else, OR to remove the Confederate battle flag from the statehouse dome,
but move it to a monument or other place of honor on the statehouse grounds, OR
to keep the Confederate battle flag flying over the statehouse dome?

	Whites (%)	Blacks (%)
Remove flag	15	37
Move to Memorial	49	50
Leave flag up	31	6
Don't know (volunteered)	4	7
	(457)	(162)

Source: Mason-Dixon Political-Media Research, Inc.

Notes: Sample is likely November voters in South Carolina. The survey was in the field
January 18–19, 2000.

variable should capture the additional (and countervailing) effect for blacks
of living in a heavily black county. Given the dichotomous dependent variable (holding one's position versus moving to the middle position),[6] we analyze the data via logistic regression.

Table 3.2 shows a significant asymmetry in the relationship between race
and movement toward compromise, specifically, the relationship we hypoth-
esized. Black flag opponents are more likely than white flag proponents to
move to the middle position, with the coefficient associated with the respondents' race achieving statistical significance almost at the .01 level. The only
other variable to achieve statistical significance is sex: women are more
likely to move to the compromise than men. Moreover, while the coefficients
linked to racial balance do not achieve significance, the relationships are in
the direction that group conflict theory would predict. In particular, the

Table 3.2. An Asymmetrical Response to the Flag Compromise

	Logit	SE
Black respondents	.72**	(.31)
Female	.39*	(.22)
Age	−.07	(.24)
Percent black	−.12	(.35)
Percent black × black respondents	.30	(.11)
Constant	−.60**	(.30)

$N = 358$
Cox Snell $R^2 = .06$

$^* p < .10$ $^{**} p < .05$ $^{***} p < .01$

Note: This analysis is confined to white flag proponents and black flag opponents. The dependent variable is whether or not a respondent moves from one of the polar positions to the compromise position in the follow-up question.

coefficient for "percent black" can be interpreted as how whites respond to living among more blacks: they become less likely to compromise. On the other hand, the interaction coefficient (viewed in the context of its constituent terms) suggests that blacks become more likely to compromise if they live among more blacks.

The asymmetry we see here is striking in the context of other studies that show that middle positions generally draw roughly equal numbers of respondents from two polar positions when survey questions are structured this way (Presser and Schuman 1980). This study is slightly different in that the middle category is not the status quo as it is in Stanley Presser and Howard Schuman's experiments. Nonetheless, in that study, and in this one, the middle category represents the middle ground, and the asymmetry in the relationship suggests that the efforts to reach compromise must overcome more resistance from whites threatened by change.

Two Dimensions of the Political Process

Our normative interest in this project is to understand how white hostility toward black political interests can be eased. In this particular situation, the question is whether flag proponents can be encouraged to accept political compromise in larger numbers, especially in light of the asymmetry just discussed. This, it would seem, has all kinds of benefits for a place like South

Carolina. In this section, we look at two dimensions of the political process to see if highlighting them can bring more whites to accept the Confederate flag outcome in South Carolina.

One such dimension is the negotiation process itself. While *compromise* might connote an abandonment of principles for some, might it also be seen in a positive light? Can the very fact that leaders of each side in a political conflict have come together to relinquish hard-line competitive positions and to bargain and negotiate for a resolution have an impact on the positions of flag proponents? Can an official resolution of group conflict affect the conflict-informed attitudes of some in the mass public?

The political process also requires majorities to be constructed and power to be asserted. Much of the group-related thinking that leads to white opposition to black political interests is a function of how people think about majorities and minorities (Glaser 1994). In the South Carolina context, many whites value majority status, as it is some justification for many of the political advantages they have. One sees this throughout the Confederate flag debate, with the most vocal flag leaders calling for a referendum to resolve the issue, not just to avoid making a tough decision, but surely because majority rule is easier to live by where one's group, on issue after issue, has the advantage. But what about those situations where the other side has built a majority through the political process? What if a coalition of blacks and whites constitute a majority on an issue, at least a majority on behalf of political compromise? We placed an item on the first Mason-Dixon survey and found that almost 70 percent of flag proponents believe that a majority of their fellow citizens stood with their hard-line position, while only 10 percent believe they stand in a minority.[7] If this (mis)perception of flag proponents is broken, will they find this a compelling reason to accept the compromise? Is there some grudging respect for the construction of a majority in the political process, especially among those in a competitive context who often take refuge in majority status?

Here, we test two propositions stemming from these group conflict questions, what we call the negotiated compromise hypothesis and the majority for compromise hypothesis. In both cases, we investigate whether highlighting these aspects of the political process changes more minds among flag proponents. In order to test these two hypotheses, we rely upon public opinion experiments placed on a second Mason-Dixon survey that was in the field just two weeks after the first. Governor Hodges had spent these two weeks in well-publicized deliberations with all the parties and was about to announce his plan to the public (the survey wrapped up the day before Hodges's announcement). Because of the timing of the survey—a few weeks prior to the Republican presidential primary in the state—the sample only contains Republicans. While this has a downside in that the results do not generalize to the complete voting population of South Carolina, they do generalize to a large proportion of white voters in the state (almost three-quarters of voters in presidential elections; Moreland and Steed 1997, 117) and a swath of the electorate that is most likely to be pro-flag (recall that a 1994 referendum of Republican primary voters supported the capitol flag by a ratio of three to one). Indeed, the Republican sample allowed us to amass a larger number of flag proponents to spread over the two treatments.

The survey experiment employed to test these two hypotheses repeats the two-pronged question discussed above. As before, respondents are anchored by the first question asking their initial opinion on the flag issue. This part of the question remains unchanged. In these experiments, however, respondents to the survey are randomly placed into one of two treatments on the second question, both treatments variations on the question asked in the first survey. To test the negotiated compromise hypothesis, we changed the compromise category in the second part of the question from the option "to remove the Confederate battle flag from the statehouse dome, but move it to a monument or other place of honor on the statehouse grounds" to "*A political compromise negotiated by black and white leaders* to remove the Confederate battle flag," offering nothing to the imagination about the source of the compromise. To test the majority for compromise hypothesis, respondents in the other half of the sample were offered yet another middle category, "*A compromise supported by a majority of South Carolinians* to remove the Confederate battle flag." In each case, the wording of this middle response category is the only thing that is altered. Comparing the responses to these two questions to each other and to the original question allows for a test of how highlighting these different dimensions of politics might affect how flag proponents respond to the compromise.[8]

In analyzing how these two changes in response category affect the responses of flag proponents, we look at the percentage moving to compromise in the two treatments (majority for compromise, and negotiated compromise). We also compare this to the percentage moving to compromise in the original question (the baseline condition). Thus, there are three statistical

Table 3.3. Flag Proponents Move Differentially to Compromise Depending on Which Aspect of Politics Is Emphasized

	Baseline	Majority for compromise	Negotiated compromise
Percent moving to compromise	.35	.43[a]	.34[a]
	(219)	(182)	(170)
t	—	1.69*	.33
	* $p < .10$	** $p < .05$	*** $p < .01$

[a] The difference between these means is significant ($t = 1.91$, $p < .06$).

Source: Mason-Dixon Political-Media Research, Inc.

Notes: The first survey was in the field January 18–19, 2000. The second survey was in the field February 14–15, 2000. The first survey sampled all likely November voters. The second survey was of likely Republican voters only. Analysis is restricted to white flag proponents from both surveys. Cells represent the proportion of respondents who move to compromise in the control condition and in each of the treatment conditions.

Question wording:

Baseline: Which of the following options would you prefer? To remove the Confederate battle flag from the statehouse dome and not display it anywhere else, OR to remove the Confederate battle flag from the statehouse dome, but move it to a monument or other place of honor on the statehouse grounds, OR to keep the Confederate battle flag flying over the statehouse dome?

Majority for compromise: Exactly the same as Q2 except for the following wording. [A compromise supported by a majority of South Carolinians] to remove the Confederate battle flag from the statehouse dome, but move it to a monument or other place of honor on the statehouse grounds, OR

Negotiated compromise: Exactly the same as Q2 except for the following wording. [A political compromise negotiated by black and white leaders] to remove the Confederate battle flag from the statehouse dome, but move it to a monument or other place of honor on the statehouse grounds, OR

tests at hand: we compare the two questions on survey 2 to each other, and we compare each to the "neutral" question asked on survey 1.

The negotiated compromise hypothesis fails here. Flag proponents in this treatment are not more likely to accept the compromise than if they are not given any "political information" about the middle category. The majority for compromise hypothesis, however, does receive some support. The likelihood of moving to compromise in this condition is almost ten points greater than in the original condition or the negotiated compromise condition. Being told that they are in a minority in the state, breaking the impression of majority status (a wrong impression, according to these surveys), leads more flag proponents over the compromise line.

The finding that negotiated compromise does not seem to matter to flag proponents may be disappointing but from a group conflict perspective, it is not surprising.[9] Good faith negotiations may appeal to those who believe that differences can be overcome with reason and empathy. The mere fact of negotiation and compromise, however, does not adjust or alter the underlying basis of white hostility to black interests. The prescription is not tied to the diagnosis. The building of a majority, on the other hand, is an assertion of power. While this may not be the most virtuous reason to accept racial change, ultimately motivations matter less than outcomes. Here again is some suggestion of how politics can change white minds, even on an emotional and symbolic issue that tangibly represents a larger conflict between white heritage and black grievance, such as the clash over the flag.

Following Neighbors, If Not Leaders

Laws are sometimes compared to sausages. For both, so goes the line, "it is better not to know how they are made." Perhaps this is true for sausages, but need it always be true for laws and policies? Does political process have to turn people off? Certainly there is much about process that many find disillusioning, even upsetting. But we argue generally (here and elsewhere in this book) that there are also aspects of the process that have the potential to work otherwise and that we can look to process in addressing some of our racial controversies. We can practice politics in such a way as to reduce white hostility toward blacks. The key to this, we argue, is understanding that the origin of some white hostility to blacks is inherently political and stems from group competition and conflict. This is an important lesson that resonates well beyond South Carolina's borders.

In this chapter, we show that the political compromise appears to have influenced the South Carolina public. Many people, black and white, came to accept the compromise as the process moved forward. We show that some people responded to it more than others, that black flag opponents were more likely to move to compromise than white flag proponents, as one would expect given a group conflict understanding of racial politics. Further, we examine how acceptance of the compromise depends on its source. Does just any compromise increase support? No. We find evidence that the cue must come from the people, rather than elites, to be effective, from neighbors, not just leaders. The exercise yields some insight into how and why process might lead people to embrace compromise—a matter about which we will have more to say in the closing chapter.

Coda

The leadership of the NAACP was unhappy with the flag compromise and refused to call off its boycott, though many black leaders in the state expressed satisfaction with the outcome. Some southern heritage groups felt their position had been abandoned and since have rallied periodically against the compromise. Most politicians, however, have declared victory and moved on. The status quo had been altered, and that is often very tough to accomplish. South Carolina seems to have accepted the outcome on the flag.[10]

Other things happened in the state as a result of the Confederate flag controversy. As the flag process was nearing an end, South Carolina's state legislature passed a bill designating Martin Luther King Day as a state holiday. In the same bill, the legislature created Confederate Heroes Day, yet another state holiday. Also, a new African American history monument, a sculpture with twelve panels depicting moments in South Carolina black history, was constructed on statehouse grounds at this time. From the black history monument, one now can see the Confederate monument and new flag display. Although it is at a busy intersection, the Confederate monument is well protected from the wind and the flag frequently lies limp and hidden from view.

CHAPTER 4

Remorse, Retribution, and Restoration

In 1988, the U.S. Congress issued an apology and authorized a $20,000 payment to each American citizen of Japanese ancestry who had been interned in detention camps during World War II. Momentous as this gesture was for those who had been in the camps, it was an extraordinary moment in the country's history as it was the most direct apology ever issued by the federal government to a domestic minority group and the first time ever an apology from the U.S. government would come with a payment of reparation. President Reagan himself expressed the apology when signing the bill authorizing payments to the 60,000 living Japanese American citizens who had been detained during the war. Said the president at the signing ceremony, "What is most important in this bill has less to do with property than with honor. For here we admit wrong" (quoted in Nelson 1988).

The internment apology may have been part of a grander trend. By some measures, we have become a more remorseful society, both inside and outside of Washington. Aaron Lazare (2004) traces an increase in apologies in professional circles—physicians apologizing to patients for mistakes, for instance—as well as in popular culture: more books, advice columns, and television shows related to apologies. Journalists have noticed an increase in apologies by public figures, identifying "an orgy of apologies spreading across the world" (O'Connor 2004, p. L1; see also Fallow 2005).

Looking systematically at news coverage over time bolsters this impression. Starting in 1980, Figure 4.1 tracks the number of *New York Times* articles that mention "apology" or "apologize" in the headline or lead paragraph. The trend line starts to climb following the congressional apology to Japanese American internees and reaches a new sustained level, almost twice the previous level, in the 1990s and 2000s. The pattern is not just a function of a larger

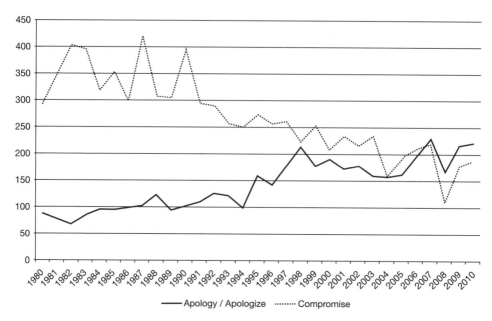

Figure 4.1. Apologies on the Rise
Figure shows the number of *New York Times* stories mentioning "apology" or "apologize" versus "compromise" in the headline or lead paragraph, by year. Results based on Lexis Nexis searches.

denominator (more stories in the *Times*) or a general softening of society. As Figure 4.1 shows, the trend for "compromise," which functions as either a noun or a verb, is quite clearly in the opposite direction.[1] There appears to be something more genuinely apologetic in our societal discourse in recent decades.

In some respects, the cascade of apologies seems to be reflected in thinking about the exploitation of blacks. Acting independently, religious denominations such as the Southern Baptists, the Moravians, and the Episcopalians have offered formal apologies and ceremonies of remorse for their past discriminatory policies and the participation of their leadership in supporting slavery and Jim Crow laws, as has the Archdiocese of New Orleans. Professional organizations like the American Medical Association and the American Dental Association and universities such as University of Virginia and Emory University have also passed resolutions of apology through their membership, faculty, or trustees.

Governments, too, have participated in this trend. For instance, there has been a spate of enthusiasm for state-level disclosure laws. State legislatures in California, Illinois, and Iowa, and city governments in Chicago, Los Angeles, Detroit, and Philadelphia required firms to investigate and reveal their past role in slavery in order to do business with the government. Particularly vulnerable were banks that financed the purchase of slaves or took slaves as collateral, and insurance companies that issued property insurance for slaves, paid claims for escapees, or offered rewards to bounty hunters to bring back escapees. Many of these firms discovered that, in their growth over the decades, they had acquired competitors that had fully participated in the economic undergirding of slavery. The disclosure laws thus exposed ties to the past and evoked apologies from firms such as Wachovia Bank, Aetna Insurance, J. P. Morgan Chase, and Bank of America.

Disclosure laws are, in one sense, easy for politicians and the public generally to endorse because they only require *others* to admit wrongdoing. Nevertheless, there has been a flurry of instances in which governments themselves have issued apologies for participating in and supporting slavery and discrimination. Perhaps the most extraordinary of these occurred when, in 2007, Governor Bob Riley signed a resolution of apology in the capitol building in Montgomery, Alabama, the very same place that served as the first capital of the Confederacy. In addition to Alabama, formal apologies for supporting slavery (and in some cases, segregation) have been passed by state legislators and signed by governors in Virginia, Maryland, North Carolina, Florida, and even New Jersey. In 2008, the U.S. House of Representatives passed a resolution (H. Res. 194) officially apologizing for slavery, stating that "confession of the wrongs committed can speed racial healing and reconciliation and help Americans confront the ghosts of their past." The Senate followed suit with a similar resolution a year later (S. Con. Res. 26).

So there has been a profound and important trend toward governmental apologies to wronged groups. For governments to win support not only for apologies, but for actual recompense, however, appears to be a greater challenge. True, the U.S. government did pay out reparations to American citizens interned in the Japanese relocation camps, but even that result is notable for how long and how difficult the process of obtaining the payments became. Few now remember that, even once the apology was offered and the payments authorized, it was still two years before Congress appropriated any money to follow through. Over the course of these two years, there was great uncertainty about whether the payouts would actually occur, and it was only the sustained effort of Representative Norman Mineta, Senator Alan K. Simpson, and the Japanese American Citizens League that completed the process. In the course of those two years, 1,600 of the 60,000 internees passed away without having received the payment from the government. As for slavery, to date, the federal government has not issued any payments. Indeed, the 2009 Senate resolution of apology contained a stark disclaimer that nothing in it "authorizes or supports" claims against the United States.

There are many reasons to expect that societal gestures of remorse like reparations will be difficult to achieve through political processes. Lazare (1995) remarks that apologies involve an actual exchange, an "exchange of shame and power" (p. 42). The politics of reparations are so vexed because through the political process, this exchange enters a group conflict frame. Groups are perceived to be winners and losers. Stakes that are otherwise distant and abstract materialize and become easier to understand. Even token concessions can become swollen with symbolism. Moreover, difficult questions abound on who should be considered wronged and who should be considered responsible. Should contemporary people bear the cost of making amends for injustices perpetrated by their ancestors? How about individuals descended from those who took no part in the offense, or even opposed it (e.g., for slavery, the descendants of abolitionists, or recent immigrants)? With many injustices littering American history, does making reparations to one group open a Pandora's box?

For these same reasons, it should also be unsurprising that reparations for blacks are extraordinarily unpopular with whites in public opinion surveys. Indeed, reparations are among the least popular public policies there are. Compare national support for reparations with support for other policies that we know are often rejected by the American public and by whites in particular. Less than 15 percent of the public supports "reparations for slavery" or "cash payments to black Americans who are descendants of slaves." This puts support for reparations at about the level of support for foreign aid, a long-standing, notoriously unpopular expenditure of public funds. Reparations are even less popular than welfare or congressional pay raises, two other policies that have long generated hostility from the public (Table 4.1).

Given how unpopular reparations are, efforts at reparations can seem quixotic and politically out of reach. This chapter argues that such actions need not be so unpopular, that there are ways to frame them and to pursue them that make them more acceptable to the public in general and whites

Table 4.1. Public Support for Reparations Is Low Even When Compared to Other Unpopular Government Expenditures

	All	Whites	Blacks
Reparations 2002	14/81	6/90	55/37
% should/should not	(1,012)	(810)	(107)
Reparations 2001	11/81		
% yes/no	(905)		
Foreign aid 2004	12/45	9/48	19/37
% increased/decreased	(1,184)	(835)	(181)
Foreign aid 2002	8/56	6/57	3/55
% too little/too much	(1,402)	(1,023)	(154)
Welfare 2004	23/32	20/33	35/27
% increased/decreased	(1,180)	(836)	(176)
Congressional pay raise	24/74		
% approve/disapprove	(1,031)		

Question wording:

Reparations 2002 (CNN/USA Today/Gallup) Do you think the government should or should not make cash payments to black Americans who are descendants of slaves? 1) should 2) should not 3) no opinion (not reported in above table)

Reparations 2001 (Fox News/Opinion Dynamics): Do you think the United States should pay reparations for slavery, that is, pay money to African Americans who are descendants of slaves? 1) yes 2) no 3) not sure (not reported in above table)

Foreign aid 2004 and Welfare 2004 (American National Election Studies): I am going to read you a list of federal programs. For each one, I would like you to tell me whether you would like to see spending increased or decreased. What about welfare/foreign aid. Should federal spending on welfare/foreign aid be increased, decreased, or kept about the same? ("kept about the same" and volunteered "cut out entirely" not reported in above table)

Foreign aid 2002 (Washington Post/Kaiser Family Foundation/Harvard University): Turning to the issue of foreign aid, do you think the United States is now spending too little on foreign aid, about the right amount, or too much on foreign aid? ("about the right amount" and volunteered "don't know" not reported in the above table)

Congressional pay raise 1999 (Pew Research Center for the People and the Press): As you may know, the U.S. House of Representatives recently voted to increase the pay of members of Congress from approximately $137,000 to approximately $141,000. Do you approve or disapprove of this pay raise? (volunteered "no opinion" not reported in above table)

in particular. The key, we argue, is to take them out of the group conflict context by framing them as *retributive* rather than *restorative* justice. We make this argument with insights derived from a particular case, the unsuccessful pursuit of reparations in conjunction with an apology in Oklahoma in the early 2000s, where we placed survey experiments in a series of commercial public opinion surveys.[2]

Symbolic gestures like apologies and reparations can be powerful and consequential, potentially facilitating healing and cooperation after periods of conflict.[3] As Melissa Nobles (2008) notes, they change our understanding of the past, including which events we should avoid repeating and which can justify present and future conduct. Yet very little scholarship has systematically examined the underpinnings of public opinion about apologies and reparations. The results from these experiments provide support for the idea that opposition to reparations stems at least partially from the perception of racial competition, and suggest ways to influence how people think about reparations, and presumably about other issues of race as well.

The 1921 Riot in Oklahoma and Its Aftermath

Following World War I, America experienced a period of significant racial turmoil and strife, one of many such periods in American history but a significant one nonetheless. The roots of the strife lay in the war. While American involvement in the conflict was relatively brief, the war effort required African American participation and the country's black leadership encouraged patriotic support. During the war years, blacks contributed $250 million in Liberty Loans (Cronon 1969, 27–28). More important, many joined the military, some in combat roles, and overall, blacks comprised more than 9 percent of U.S. military personnel during the war (Klinkner and Smith 1999, 111). Fighting for their country and for the principles of freedom and democracy raised expectations, both among black veterans and their families back home. As W. E. B. Du Bois wrote in *Crisis*: "We *return*. We *return from fighting*. We *return fighting*. Make way for Democracy! We saved it in France, and by the Great Jehovah, we will save it in the U.S.A., or know the reason why" (Franklin and Moss 1994, 316–317).

If black expectations were rising in the years following the war, so was white resistance, in the South and throughout the country. During the war, unprecedented opportunities in industry and a campaign to advertise these opportunities to southern blacks pulled 400,000 migrants out of the South (Marks 1989), contributing to a peak period in the Great Migration (Lemann 1991). The combination of discharged white military personnel returning to their jobs and homes, a changed racial balance in their home environments, an economic recession exacerbated by the contraction of war industries, and a black population that had new expectations made for a brew of resentment

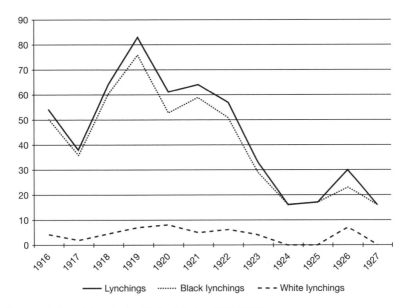

Figure 4.2. Lynchings in the United States 1917–1926
Source: Lynching Records at Tuskegee Institute (Williams 1970)

and anger. One manifestation of the rise in racial resentment among whites was the revival and growth of the Ku Klux Klan. By early 1921, the Klan was adding chapters and members at a remarkable rate (McVeigh 2009). In another measure of the racial resentment in this period, lynching, though not as commonplace as in earlier eras, was reemerging as a tool of intimidation and oppression. In the five years following the war, the country experienced a crest in lynching, with blacks almost exclusively the victims (Figure 4.2). Looking at this period through the lens of group conflict theory, it is not surprising that heightened competition for space, housing, and employment and different expectations of whites and blacks would lead to an environment of mistrust, terror, and fear, all of which contributed to the events in Tulsa in 1921, one of the most devastating race riots in American history.

The precipitating event for the riot was an interracial encounter in a downtown Tulsa building. It was Memorial Day, and a young black man named Dick Rowland was shining shoes for people gathered for a holiday parade. Seeking a restroom located on the top floor of the building he was working from, Rowland took an elevator. On his way down, he found himself alone with Sarah Page, a young white woman. According to one history of the event, it is not clear whether Rowland and Page knew each other or even were involved in some sort of relationship (Brophy 2002). And what exactly happened in the elevator is also unclear. What is clear is that a clerk from the department store on the building's first floor heard the girl scream and saw the boy run out of the elevator. The version of events described in the *Tulsa Tribune* had Rowland attacking Page in the elevator, tearing at her clothes, scratching her face, and perhaps attempting to rape her. The following morning, Rowland was arrested and taken into custody at the county courthouse jail. This, of course, was the most provocative kind of incident in that era, one that tapped into the worst thoughts, stereotypes, and dreads of southern whites. It was also the type of incident that could precipitate a lynching,[4] and indeed it is believed that an editorial in the next day's Tulsa newspaper either called for a lynching or speculated that one was in the making (Ellsworth 2001).

Over the course of the following day, talk of a lynching spread across the city and a white mob gathered at the county courthouse. Inside the courthouse, the sheriff, alarmed, put provisions into place to protect Dick Rowland. He was right to do so. The year before, under a different sheriff, a mob had raided the courthouse and, with little resistance from law enforcement, taken away and lynched a prisoner. Perhaps motivated by that embarrassment, the sheriff gave strict instructions to beat back the mob should they try to raid the jail.

In Greenwood, a black neighborhood across the railroad tracks from the white section of town, there was also talk of whites gathering at the courthouse. Concerned, the community's leadership decided to mobilize, and within short order, a group of black leaders and war veterans, armed, traveled to the courthouse and announced to the assembled crowd their intention to defend the jail and the prisoner. The sheriff asked them to return home, and they did, but their presence, and the threat of black violence, alarmed the gathered whites. Some went home for their own guns, while others attempted to break into the National Guard armory for weapons and ammunition. Over the course of the day, the crowd in front of the courthouse swelled to more than two thousand restive people. Later in the evening, the black leaders returned to the courthouse, again declaring their intent to defend the black prisoner. Once more, they were discouraged by the sheriff, but as they were leaving the scene this time, there was a skirmish that led to a shot being fired. This sparked a short but lethal confrontation. The blacks, outnumbered, retreated, with several losing their lives. Enraged, whites gathered in front of the police station and over five hundred of them, remarkably, were deputized by the city police directing this operation and instructed to "get a gun and get a nigger" (Ellsworth 2001, 64).

Shortly, a full-scale riot engulfed the city. While a gun battle straddled the railroad tracks dividing white and black Tulsa, looting, arson, and shooting occurred throughout the city with a very limited response by Tulsa's police. A National Guard unit was activated to restore order, but many of the guardsmen believed that they were to quell a "black uprising" and rounded up Greenwood's blacks, who were then interned at the police station. Those who resisted were shot. This had the effect of leaving black homes and businesses vulnerable to looting and arson, and the next morning, five to ten thousand whites "invaded" Greenwood (Ellsworth 2001, 71). Police, deputies, and national guardsmen participated in the atrocities. Firefighters, threatened at gunpoint, failed to put out fires in the black district and instead worked to keep the fires from spreading to the white part of town. There also were reports of airplanes flying overhead dropping dynamite on Greenwood, evidence to some people of an effort by authorities to punish the black population for challenging whites at the courthouse. In the end, thirty-five square blocks in the city were turned to rubble, up to 150 people (perhaps more) were killed, and more than a thousand families were left homeless (Brophy 2001, 44, 60). It was not just that the riot was devastating; the negligence of city officials in protecting black Tulsans made this incident especially appalling.

In the aftermath, nearly all of the survivors of the riot were in custody. Within a week, they were released, but there was nothing much to return to. For those who stayed in Tulsa, a tent city went up, and with some assistance from the Red Cross, people survived. The infrastructure in the Greenwood district was decimated, and many of those who survived the riot left Tulsa, never to return. As James Hirsch, a chronicler of the riot, has written, this conflict set new standards of destruction and "resulted in the liquidation of virtually an entire black community and the institutions that held it together. It was reminiscent of the pogroms of czarist Russia and an omen of the ethnic cleansing that would, decades hence, sear central Africa and the Balkans" (Hirsch 2002, 120).

The riot itself was not the end of the travesty for the black community. The official response to the riot was unfriendly and gave little hope for assistance in rebuilding. Indeed, the grand jury that met the following month to investigate the events surrounding the riots placed the blame for the riot on the black leaders who had gone to the courthouse to defend the imprisoned

Dick Rowland. As the Tulsa newspaper reported it, "Grand Jury Blames Negroes for Inciting Race Rioting: Whites Clearly Exonerated" (Brophy 2001). There were seventy indictments from the grand jury, directed predominantly at blacks. Most were dropped later in the year, after Dick Rowland's case was dismissed when Sarah Page failed to appear in court (Brophy 2001). The police chief was fined and fired for his role in the episode, but it does not appear that anyone, black or white, served time for their role in the riots, and clearly justice was not done (Madigan 2001).

Likewise, lawsuits filed after the riots came to naught. Over two hundred lawsuits were filed against the city, insurance companies, and the Sinclair Oil Company (which some believed to have provided the airplanes that allegedly bombed Greenwood), but only one of them was successful, that by a white hardware store owner whose shop was looted for guns by white rioters (Nelson 1999). The insurance policies had riot exclusion clauses, which the courts recognized, and by 1937, all the suits were defunct.

In the immediate wake of the riot came condemnation from around the country. Editorialists in countless newspapers called Tulsa a national disgrace, a horror, and a "name of shame." The riot became a source of great embarrassment, and the city responded logically, shoving the event into what might be called the closet of history, where it could be conveniently forgotten. Over time, it was. The riot was not taught in schools, mentioned in the media, or commemorated in any way. Twenty-five years after the riot, the city's newspaper did not even mention it in the "Twenty-Five Years Ago Today" column. "It was," wrote John Hope Franklin and Scott Ellsworth (2001, 26), "as if the greatest catastrophe in the city's history simply had not happened at all."[5]

The Effort to Redress Historical Wrongs

In April 1995, a horrendous act of domestic terrorism struck Oklahoma City. One hundred and sixty-eight people, including nineteen children in a day-care center, perished when the Alfred P. Murrah Federal Building collapsed after it was bombed by disaffected Army veteran Timothy McVeigh. The attention to the victims of the crime, its origins, and its broader implications for society was extraordinary. So too was the outpouring of support that flowed into Oklahoma City. Not surprisingly, the response from the political class was immediate and substantial, leading to several important pieces of legislation regarding terrorism and security.

Highlighting the state's capacity for action and the comparatively anemic response to the Tulsa riots, then approaching their seventy-fifth anniversary, Representative Don Ross, a former civil rights activist whose constituency was heavily black and whose district included what was once Greenwood (and is now a freeway), introduced a reparations bill in the state legislature. Ross's bill would grant reparations from the state to those who suffered losses in the riots and to their descendants. The bill authorized $5 million in direct compensation for losses and an additional $1 million to support children's programs, intended as a gesture toward those in future generations who were affected by the change in the trajectory of their community. Ross certainly recognized that the chances of his bill passing were low. As he told a Tulsa reporter, "If I believed my bill would pass, I would be deluding myself and the public. But as long as I am in the legislature, it will be an issue that they will have to reject. So, I will introduce it every year as long as I serve" (Underwood 1997).

As he expected, Ross's effort to provide reparations failed in the legislature, but his colleagues did do something in response to the bill, a first attempt at understanding the riot and acknowledging past wrongs. Ross's bill was amended to commission a study on the riots and to make recommendations on how amends could be made. The legislature even appropriated $50,000 to fund the commission. It was either a first step toward reparations or a way to deflect the issue, but much depended upon the case the multiracial commission would build. The commissioners first sought to establish a more accurate calculation of the riot's casualties, given that the official count at the time was clearly understated. They also sought to get a better picture of the state of the community and economy in North Tulsa. How many people were victims of the riot? What was lost? How culpable were city, county, and state officials? The answers to these questions were considered to be critical in deciding who should receive reparations and what form they should take.

Three years later, in early 2000, the commission made its recommendations to the state legislature in a preliminary report (the official report was issued in 2001). The commission's findings were striking. Most important, the commission identified seventy additional living survivors of the riot, critical given the perceived need to identify people who were directly harmed in 1921. In addition to its extensive fact-finding, the commission recommended payments to living survivors and to the descendants of those who lost property in the riot, a scholarship fund, an "enterprise zone" to promote economic development in North Tulsa, and a memorial to the victims of the riot. It was time, said the report, for the state to recognize that it had "moral responsibilities" to pay reparations "to fully acknowledge and finally discharge a collective responsibility" (Goble 2001, 19–20).

As the commission completed its business, the two commissioners who were state legislators were not very optimistic about how the recommendations would be treated by their legislative colleagues. The Democratic legislator believed that while scholarships might have a chance at passage, reparations were highly unlikely, given that city and county officials, not state officials, were more blameworthy in 1921, and given that so much time had passed. "Restitution for survivors is iffy," he said to a reporter, "I say that because I've had a lot of people say, 'Where does it stop?'" (Krehbiel 2000). And the Republican lawmaker on the commission raised similar concerns: "What about the other situations where people had losses because of actions by prejudiced people? The chances [of it passing the legislature] are very slim. This was a long time ago" (Romano 2000, A3). Raising the issue of how much today's citizens owe to correct past wrongs, Oklahoma's governor Frank Keating commented on the bill: "Compensation for direct loss occasioned by direct state or city action is not inappropriate. But it has to be shown that there was real harm to existing, living individuals and that direct action by the city and the state caused the harm. . . . It's going to be a very slippery slope to climb [to support] using current taxpayers' money to compensate for the acts of past taxpayers" (Romano 2000).

True to expectations, the legislature again failed to support reparations, though notably they mostly accepted the findings of the commission. Instead of reparations, the legislature passed a symbolic bill that blamed the riot on white racists and condemned the "conspiracy of silence" surrounding the event. The legislation also established a scholarship fund, provided seed money for a memorial and a Greenwood museum, and provided each survivor with an Oklahoma Medal of Distinction, though the medals were paid for by private contributions and not state funds. The bill passed narrowly, with opponents objecting to official and explicit blame assigned to white Tulsans. In the wake of this legislative activity, a private effort by Tulsa clergy to provide reparations raised $28,000 to disburse to 131 living survivors of the riot. While $214.03 was inadequate to compensate for the losses that victims suffered, the leader of the effort called the payments "a gift from the religious community that acknowledges the need for reparations" (Krehbiel 2002).

The reparations effort did not end there, however. It moved to a courtroom after attracting the attention of prominent African American attorneys from outside the state. In early 2003, Harvard law professor Charles Ogletree and Johnnie Cochran, who had successfully defended O. J. Simpson, brought together a team to push for reparations in the courts, filing lawsuits on behalf of three hundred plaintiffs (roughly one hundred survivors and two hundred descendants) against the state of Oklahoma and the city of Tulsa. As the case made its way through the court system, the critical issue was not whether reparations were due to the plaintiffs, but whether the statute of limitations applied to the situation. Did the discovery of new evidence, purposely concealed or destroyed in the years after the event, justify a re-setting of the clock? Unfortunately for the plaintiffs, a district court ruled and an appellate court affirmed that it did not. In May 2005, when the Supreme Court declined to hear a final appeal, the case was dead.

Retributive Versus Restorative Justice

In the middle of the reparations effort in Oklahoma, law professor Alfred Brophy wrote that the situation there provided "a laboratory in which to test ideas about reparations, to ask the question, can justice be done?" (2002, xx). In the end, nothing much was done. We argue, however, that there are some lessons embedded in the quest for justice in Tulsa. The most important of them, from our perspective, is that it matters how one conceives and characterizes this term.

Two frameworks for thinking about legal resolution, often pitted as alternatives, seem quite relevant to thinking about reparations. We argue that one of them—the less idealistic of them—has the potential to resonate more with the public as people construct opinions. *Retributive justice* is the basis for much of our legal and judicial system. Its focus is on *desert*, the appropriate relationship between a transgression and restitution, on what will make the victim whole. The process of justice delivery is objective, managed and settled by a judge, jury, or other authority, and designed to assure fairness and evenhandedness. *Restorative justice* is a newer and perhaps less familiar concept. Its primary focus is on the process of healing—of the victim, but also of the offender and the larger community. Its ideal is a negotiated consensus as to what happened, what the shared values are, and what actions—which may or may not involve punishment and compensation—will allow everyone to move forward (Wenzel et al. 2008).

Three distinctions between retributive and restorative justice are especially relevant to our discussion. The first has to do with the presence of apology. While remorse is occasionally expressed in retributive processes, acceptance of responsibility and apologies are not sufficient or even necessary components of retributive justice. It requires addressing specific wrongs with specific penalties or appropriate remuneration, but sentiment need not be part of the equation. On the other hand, acknowledgment, apology, and agreement are often integral parts of the restorative justice ideal. Resolution of conflict comes with the return of the victim's dignity, and even the transgressor experiences some moral cleansing by participating in the process. The transgressor accepts responsibility for the offending actions and the victim demonstrates a willingness to forgive and move on.

Second, social psychologists show that retributive justice, more than restorative justice, is likely to resonate where groups are in conflict. Without a sense of some greater unity—a sense of shared community or superordinate identity to bring people together—restorative processes have less chance of success. In contrast, distinct groups are more likely to endorse rules and concepts (like retribution) that allow them to get by, if not to get along.

Third, psychological research shows that certain attitudes associated with conservatism such as deference to authority, a stronger endorsement of individualism, and a positive orientation toward tradition (Graham, Haidt, and Nosek 2009) lead to greater support for retributive justice. One can see how this would be the case. Retributive justice involves the imposition of punishment from some authority, and its concern with "just deserts" means that individual transgressors and specific victims, not groups more broadly defined, are the focus. Furthermore, restorative justice has a kind of "Kumbaya" quality. Take for example legal scholar Martha Minow's words, "Restorative justice emphasizes the humanity of both offenders and victims. It seeks repair of social connections and peace rather than retribution against the offenders" (1998, 92). It is not hard to imagine that this concept could be anathema to those with a more conservative orientation.

Within this framework, reparations represent quintessential restorative justice. They are intended to reconcile past wrongs, but in a symbolic way. Even vigorous advocates of reparations readily acknowledge that full com-

pensation for slavery is unfeasible both because of the enormous expense—
payments could easily amount to trillions of dollars—and the practical
difficulty of identifying which blacks alive today would be owed what. But
the very fact that most reparations come from a legislature or some other
entity of the state gives them their symbolic value, as they are the result of
some political, negotiated process. Reports often accompany them, spelling
out the wrongs and embracing responsibility for them. The explicit goal is to
remember and to heal, but it is not to punish.

Nevertheless, it is difficult to generate support for reparations, and they
seem to elicit group conflict impulses. Reparations do not pit white and black
interests against each other per se. As Michael Dawson and Rovana Popoff
(2004) discuss, the philosophical justification for reparations generally rests
on the notion of corporate responsibility (the obligations of a continuing
government to its people) and not personal responsibility (payments from
whites to blacks). Yet reparations do tap into group conflict impulses, first
because the original events that require redress are racial in nature. The interpretation of racial conflict and its aftermath fits neatly into a group conflict frame. The attempt to address and redress these events years later by its
very nature means that gains due to blacks or some other minority must be
paid for by whites. Even where reparations come out of public coffers that
are filled by taxpayers of all races, the interpretation is that it is the majority
that must pay, and the gains and the losses are directly linked in people's
minds.[6] And it is not just a material gain and a material loss. The exchange
of power and shame implicit in an apology, with the majority accepting
blame and shame and the minority acquiring a power denied to them before, sets up restorative reparations as a group conflict problem.

Furthermore, most of these original events were embarrassing violations of rights that were purposefully ignored, sometimes for decades as
in Tulsa. The restorative effort must start, then, by pulling events from the
deepest recesses of societal memory. This often requires aggressive leadership from the aggrieved party, an assertiveness that is often threatening
to the majority. In Oklahoma, for instance, the fact that most leaders of
the restorative effort were black —and outsider celebrities at that—conflated
reparations with black interests more generally, likely contributing to a hostile white response.

Finally, some social psychologists have argued that support for restorative justice is very difficult to obtain where groups in more general direct
conflict are attempting to negotiate a restorative resolution. Such resolution

may be possible where the two groups have shared interests and common values, where, in the language of Michael Wenzel and colleagues (2007, 385), "the affected parties simultaneously define themselves in terms of a superordinate category that includes them all." Where that category is elusive, however, the process of negotiation and conciliation has the potential to raise the stakes of group conflict instead of resolving it.

What if reparations were framed as a form of retributive rather than restorative justice, as compensation owed for a specific wrong rather than part of a healing process? How would white opinion respond? One can imagine arguments in both directions. On the one hand, suggesting that an individual bears a responsibility to make amends for a specific wrong, rather than a distant and generalized tragedy, could be perceived as accusatory and confrontational, which could energize group conflict thinking and increase white opposition to reparations, while a "healing" frame that downplays these considerations might have the opposite effect. On the other hand, the emphasis on rules and procedures that whites generally endorse and the more familiar framework for thinking about justice could shift thinking away from group conflict. With a grievance that is perceived as concrete and legitimate, the thinking of whites may focus on degree of compensation (what would be fair?) rather than the fact of compensation (should whites make concessions or not?). We initiated our experiments with an open mind. We come out of them ready to make the case for framing reparations as a form of retributive justice.

Influencing Opinion in Oklahoma

The effort to provide reparations for the Tulsa race riots had restorative aspirations, but there were features that made the effort more retributive in nature, relative to others. Unlike reparations for slavery and Jim Crow, this was a situation where a narrowly defined set of specific and identifiable living people had been harmed in a clear and unassailable way. It was a situation where institutional racism was not an abstraction; the local government's active neglect contributed to the disaster. It was a situation where reparations were pursued in a legislative arena but also in a judicial one. Most important, in Oklahoma, the reparations became explicitly separated from the apology. Nobles (2008, 143) argues that reparations and apologies should not be considered the same thing. "At bottom," she writes, "legal and politi-

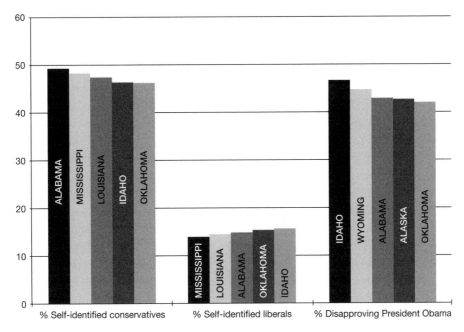

Figure 4.3. Most Conservative States, 2009
Source: Gallup surveys, http://www.gallup.com/poll/125066/State-States.aspx

cal contests over reparations follow a tort model, where the fight centers on specifying the harm(s), identifying the appropriate beneficiaries and perpetrators, and devising acceptable compensation schemes." Apologies, in contrast, "emphasize moral acknowledgment of wrongdoing" (144). In Oklahoma, this distinction became clearer over the course of the effort to win reparations, particularly as black leaders took the case to court.

Oklahoma presents a hard test for frames that generate support for reparations because its center of ideological gravity is very much to the right. In fact, Oklahoma is among the most conservative states in the nation (Figure 4.3). In 2009, the Gallup survey organization accumulated enough respondents from all fifty states to rank-order them on a long list of variables. Oklahoma was in the top five states in terms of the highest percentage of self-identified conservatives, the lowest percentage of self-identified liberals, and the highest percentage of people who disapproved of President Obama's performance. One would suspect that reparations are least likely to be popular in a place with relatively large numbers of conservative whites. If opinions on reparations can be moved in this conservative environment, our manipulations are likely to work elsewhere.

The experiments we use to test our ideas were in the field in Oklahoma in 2003, after the legislature had rejected the commission's recommendations on reparations (but passed legislation to establish scholarships and award victims the Oklahoma Medal). These experiments also were conducted after the lawsuits were filed in federal court but well before they met their demise, offering a snapshot of opinions at a moment when the issue was very much in the public eye. We placed survey experiments on two polls of Oklahoma citizens conducted in October and November 2003 by the University of Oklahoma Public Opinion Learning Laboratory (OU Poll). There were 501 respondents in the October poll and 564 in the November poll. Below, we compare questions that were asked on separate polls, which requires assuming that the intervention of time did not markedly affect attitudes. Because attention to the reparations movement had diminished by this point and no significant events intervened between the two surveys, we feel comfortable pooling the samples.

Our first experiment compares a baseline condition to two alternative frames, one of which highlights restorative considerations, the other of which highlights retributive considerations. The baseline condition substantially mimics the way questions about reparations have been asked in the past:

> Recently, there has been discussion about whether the government should pay money to African Americans for the wrongs of slavery and discrimination. Some people support these payments because they believe it is important for the government to acknowledge and apologize for its role in the suffering of blacks. Others believe that contemporary society should not have to pay for the mistakes of the past. What about you? Do you favor or do you oppose compensating African Americans for these wrongs?

In one sense, the wording of this baseline question describes the purpose of reparations for slavery and discrimination in a restorative justice frame. Acknowledgment of past wrong and remorse are the very basic elements of a restorative effort. Legal scholar Declan Roche (2003, 27) writes that "the process of reparation begins with acknowledging the harm a victim has suffered" and goes on to determine how things "can be put right." The ultimate restorative goal is societal healing, however, and the phrasing of the original

Table 4.2. Retributive, Not Restorative Frame Increases White Support

Support for reparations

	Baseline	Restorative frame	Retributive frame
All respondents	.16	.11	.24
	(221)	(269)	(227)
t	—	−1.65*	2.15**
White respondents	.08	.07	.19
	(169)	(214)	(180)
t	—	−.29	3.03***

Notes: Sample is of Oklahoma citizens (564 for the October 2003 survey and 501 for the November 2003 survey).

$^*p < .10$ $^{**}p < .05$ $^{***}p < .01$

Question wording:

Baseline frame: Recently, there has been discussion about whether the government should pay money to African Americans for the wrongs of slavery and discrimination. Some people support these payments because they believe it is important for the government to acknowledge and apologize for its role in the suffering of blacks. Others believe that contemporary society should not have to pay for the mistakes of the past. What about you? Do you favor or do you oppose compensating African Americans for these wrongs? 0) Oppose 1) Favor 2) Don't Know (missing value)

Restorative frame: Recently, there has been discussion about whether the government should pay money to African Americans for the wrongs of slavery and discrimination. Some people support these payments because they believe *these payments will help heal the racial divisions of the past.* Others believe that contemporary society should not have to pay for the mistakes of the past. What about you? Do you favor or do you oppose compensating African Americans for these wrongs? 0) Oppose 1) Favor 2) Don't Know (missing value)

Retributive frame: Recently, there has been discussion about whether the government should pay money *to those African Americans who lost loved ones and property when a white mob attacked the black community in Tulsa many years ago.* Some people support these payments because they believe it is important for the government to acknowledge and apologize for its role in the suffering of blacks. Others believe that contemporary society should not have to pay for the mistakes of the past. What about you? Do you favor or do you oppose compensating African Americans for these wrongs? 0) Oppose 1) Favor 2) Don't know (missing value)

question does not make this explicit. Thus, what we label the restorative condition highlights the healing function of reparations, replacing the phrasing "because they believe it is important for the government to acknowledge and apologize for its role in the suffering of blacks" with "because they believe these payments will help to heal the racial divisions of the past" (full question wording given in Table 4.2).

Retribution is not about a general attempt to heal society but about addressing some particular incidence of wrong, some violation of rights, or a loss of life, liberty, or property. Thus, our retributive condition shifts attention from apologies for the wrongs of slavery and discrimination in general and emphasizes the specific incident and victims at hand—African Americans who lost loved ones and property when a white mob attacked the black community in Tulsa many years ago. By shining a spotlight on a specific wrong and how it is to be righted, and by making institutional racism less abstract and more defined by specific official behavior that constitutes or contributes to the wrong, retributive reparations argumentation could be more likely to resonate with people than a general sense that contemporary society should be responsible for the mistakes of the past.

The leaders of the effort in Tulsa, and in other places where such strategies have been pursued, have started with this notion. Their purpose is not to compensate everyone descended from slavery or everyone affected by Jim Crow. Rather, they point to a very specific incident where specific people were harmed, some of whom are still alive. Will the public support reparations for such specific victims in specific circumstances? The bet of those guiding these efforts was that it would, at least enough to generate a legislative response. Our public opinion experiment also starts with this hypothesis that articulating the specific wrong, wrongdoers, and victims and emphasizing just deserts will contribute to support for compensating that wrong.

As Table 4.2 shows, support for reparations in Oklahoma at the time of our surveys, as measured in our baseline question, looks much like it does in the rest of the country: reparations "to acknowledge and apologize" for the "wrongs of slavery and discrimination" generate little support from Oklahomans. Only 16 percent of those with an opinion support reparations, while only 8 percent of whites support them. These levels of support are remarkably close to the national levels gauged in the few national surveys that happened to ask this question (see Table 4.1). This question confirms a (very low) baseline from which to measure the effect of our experimental manipulations.

We start by looking at the impact of an explicitly restorative argument on opinion. It is hard to imagine a policy that generates less support than reparations as a means to apologize, but emphasizing restorative considerations manages to do so. Only 11 percent of respondents in the restorative treatment support reparations versus 16 percent of respondents asked about reparations as an apology, a statistically significant difference. A difference in responses among whites does not emerge, but of course, support starts so low in the baseline condition that there is a floor in place. Certainly, the explicit restorative argument does not generate greater support for reparations. The goal of restorative justice does not resonate with the general public in Oklahoma. At the end of the previous section, we outlined some plausible reasons why a restorative frame might increase support for reparations, but this expectation is clearly not borne out.

The retributive condition, in contrast, does make a real difference. Respondents given this question were more likely to approve of reparations for the victims of the Tulsa riot than reparations for slavery and discrimination more generally. The differences in response are fairly large and statistically significant. Looking at all respondents, the percentage of reparations supporters increases by about half, from 16 percent in the first treatment to 24 percent in the second. Taking out blacks, Hispanics, Asians, and Native Americans, white support for specific reparations more than doubles from 8 percent to 19 percent; this is easily significant, both substantively and statistically. The outcome here illustrates that components of a retributive approach to reparations are meaningful, though sentiment on reparations still runs three-to-one against and whites are powerfully opposed, even when the reparations are targeted to specific victims.

We present the results of a second experiment that aims to build upon this finding. We hypothesize that adding other retributive elements to the equation will further build support for reparations for the Tulsa victims. We add additional retributive themes in two stages. First, an alternative frame we refer to as the "damages condition" modifies the retributive frame by asking not whether "the government should pay money" for "wrongs" but rather whether, in response to a "lawsuit," "contemporary society" should pay "damages" for "losses" (full question wording appears in Table 4.3). Note that both conditions call attention to the Tulsa riots. The difference is in characterizing recompense for the riots as a sort of symbolic gesture as opposed to damages potentially awarded in a lawsuit.

A second alternative takes one more step in modifying the damages condition. It extracts restorative themes even further by dropping references to an apology or the idea that society might pay for mistakes of the past. Absent symbolic considerations, the counterargument against reparations becomes one of a statute of limitations. With these changes, respondents are asked about reparations stripped of sentiment, and the question is fully retributive. Should black victims be treated fairly or should the case be thrown out because too much time has passed? This would be the question faced in the courts.

Our hypothesis is that highlighting retributive considerations in these ways will generate more support for reparations. The rationale here is that the judicial approach introduces a component of "just deserts" that could be meaningful. "Just deserts" pertain not only to punishment but also to compensation. It is the foundation for tort law and makes the payment a retributive transaction.

The second experiment does, in fact, generate additional support for the notion that retributive frames attenuate group conflict thinking and increase support for reparations. Table 4.3 presents the results. Shifting from the generic retributive frame to a retributive frame that uses legal terminology such as "damages" and "losses" rather than "payments" and "wrongs" (shifting from column 1 to column 2 in Table 4.3) increases overall support for reparations by 7 percentage points (a difference significant at the 0.10 level). Whites exhibit a comparable increase in support that falls a bit short of statistical significance (likely on account of the diminished sample size). For the strongest retributive frame—the frame that removes restorative considerations altogether, shown in column 3—the effects are quite clear. Overall support for reparations goes up to 45 percent, a sizable jump over the damages condition that mentions an apology, and almost double the support in the generic retributive condition. Among whites, the support generated by the new frame goes up about 15 percentage points compared to column 2 and more than doubles the support seen in column 1. The overall level of support does not reach the critical majority threshold. But it does come much closer, particularly when one considers the level of support in the baseline condition. Each step in this process further enhances a retributive approach to the problem, and with each step, progressively more support is apparent. Whether separating out the apology from the reparation makes the payments less meaningful is something we address in the conclusion. For now, we simply note that opposition to payments is neither as strong nor as obstinate as one might believe given that only about 11 percent of people support the most restorative version of the concept.

If a retributive approach to addressing past injustice is more resonant with Oklahomans, and white Oklahomans at that, is it because this approach aligns better with a more conservative, traditional approach to the world? Is it conservatives whose opinions are more likely to change as we move stepwise through the alternatives? Oklahoma is a meaningful place to look at this given that it is a more conservative and traditional place, southern in attitude and lifestyle if not completely southern by definition.[7] If our

Table 4.3. Emphasizing Retributive Considerations, Diminishing Restorative Ones, Increases Support for Reparations

Support for reparations

	Generic retributive frame (repeated from Table 4-2)	Damages with apology	Damages without apology
All respondents	.24	.31	.45
	(227)	(222)	(232)
t	—	1.63*	4.95***
White respondents	.19	.25	.40
	(180)	(170)	(167)
t	—	1.31	4.21***
	* *p* < .10	** *p* < .05	*** *p* < .01 (two-tailed)

Note: Sample is of Oklahoma citizens (564 for the October 2003 survey and 501 for the November 2003 survey).

Question wording:
For each wording, changes relative to the condition above appear in italics.

Retributive frame: Recently, there has been discussion about whether the government should pay money to African Americans for the wrongs of slavery and discrimination. Some people support these payments because they believe it is important for the government to acknowledge and apologize for its role in the suffering of blacks. Others believe that contemporary society should not have to pay for the mistakes of the past. What about you? Do you favor or do you oppose compensating African Americans for these wrongs? 0) Oppose 1) Favor 2) Don't know (missing value)

Damages frame with apology: *I'd like to ask you about a lawsuit filed here in Oklahoma. This lawsuit was filed on behalf of* those African Americans who lost loved ones and property when a white mob attacked the black community in Tulsa many years ago. Some people support *paying damages to the victims of this riot* because they believe it is important for *contemporary society* to acknowledge and apologize for *this terrible incident, even after all these years.* Other people believe that contemporary society should not have to pay for the mistakes of the past. What about you? Do you favor or do you oppose compensating African Americans *for their losses?* 0) Oppose 1) Favor 2) Don't know (missing value)

Damages condition without apology: I'd like to ask you about a lawsuit filed here in Oklahoma. This lawsuit was filed on behalf of those African Americans who lost loved ones and property when a white mob attacked the black community in Tulsa many years ago. Some people support paying damages to the victims of this riot because they believe it is important *for the black victims in this terrible incident to be treated fairly,* even after all these years. Other people believe *that blacks should not receive compensation in such an old case.* What about you? Do you favor or do you oppose compensating African Americans for their losses? 0) Oppose 1) Favor 2) Don't know (missing value) exercise changes conservative minds, then this says something about how issues like this should be approached in places like this. Of course, racial injustices were perpetrated outside the South. But there is much to apologize for in the history of the region, so understanding how conservative southern minds work on these issues has real value. There also is a theoretical reason to break down our sample by ideology. Psychologists argue that retributive justice strikes a chord with those with more conservative views. Whether because of deference to authority, a stronger embrace of individualism and a just deserts principle, a traditional brand of morality, or some combination of these things, we hypothesize that conservatives should respond more to the choices we offer in these experiments.

The Oklahoma Poll includes a five-category self-identified ideology variable in each survey, allowing us to divide our sample into conservatives and others. While there may have been some value in breaking out ideology into three categories, there are so few liberals, and white liberals in particular, in Oklahoma, that this was not a viable strategy. Nonetheless, we can compare self-described conservatives to everyone else to see if there is anything distinctive about conservative responses to our experiments.

Looking just at whites, as we do in Table 4.4, the pattern for conservatives and nonconservatives is the same, though as anticipated, conservatives respond more to the retributive approaches, particularly our final offering (paying damages to compensate for losses in the Tulsa riot). Comparing white conservatives to liberals, moderates, and others combined, they are more hostile to reparations to apologize for the Tulsa event and more hostile to paying damages to apologize for the Tulsa losses. The inter-ideological differences are substantial, if not statistically significant. Strikingly, white conservatives come to look just like everyone else in the last treatment. In the fully retributive condition, the difference between white conservatives and nonconservatives dwindles to almost nothing. The patterns are roughly the same if one looks at all respondents, not just white ones, leaving the conclusion that the shifting of the problem from a restorative to a retributive approach matters most to conservatives, as expected.

Another explanation for the impact of our retributive experiments is that the Tulsa reparations are so much smaller and less expensive than general reparations for slavery and discrimination. Perhaps it is not the retributive frame that is leading to the increase in support, but simply the change in the scope of the problem and the solution. While we agree that perceptions

Table 4.4. Retributive Justice Resonates with White Conservatives

Support for reparations	White conservatives	All other whites
Generic retributive frame	.14	.22
	(50)	(130)
t	—	1.14
Damages condition with apology	.20	.28
	(55)	(170)
t	—	1.09
Damages condition without apology	.39	.40
	(51)	(116)
t	—	.05

$^{*} p < .10$ ** $p < .05$ $^{***} p < .01$ (two-tailed)

of cost may have some bearing on how people think about reparations, there are three reasons these concerns are minimal. First, while the payments would be more focused, so, presumably, would be their cost; only Oklahoma citizens would pay for the Tulsa reparations, rather than whites nationally. For this reason, the retributive framing, in one sense, emphasizes a personal concession. Second, much work in political science finds public opinions to be rather insensitive to price tag concerns, focusing far more on symbolic concerns (Sears et al. 1980; Green 1992). Third, while the first experiment suggests differences in who would foot the bill for reparations, the second experiment holds the scope of reparations constant. Much of the growth in support of reparations is in these subsequent experiments. Something beyond scope is at work here.

Practical, If Not Virtuous

There is a real challenge in processing reparations, with their overtones of conflict and concession, through majoritarian institutions. We would expect group conflict dynamics to contribute to hostility and resistance on the part of the majority group. The findings of this chapter, however, suggest that concessions need not always generate resistance. When the concession is tied to a specific event, when it is taken through a process meant to accommodate it—in short, when it can be cast as retributive justice—resistance subsides in favor of other considerations.

The greater appeal of retributive concessions may have a real impact on which groups get what in politics. Consider how support for reparations for blacks differs from reparations directed toward Asian Americans for misdeeds committed by the United States government in World War II. The Japanese internment, because it is more recent and specific, is easier to cast in terms of retributive justice than slavery as a whole. This observation may help explain why 43 percent of whites support an apology for the internment, but only 30 percent support it for slavery. When it comes to monetary payments, the gap is even larger: 26 percent support payments to Asians versus just 4 percent supporting payments to blacks (Dawson and Popoff 2004).

Some might say that a retributive approach is less virtuous than a restorative approach. After all, it could be transformational to heal society through conciliation and agreement. But the retributive approach aligns with how many people think about justice in this country, and that is what gives retributive reparations their larger symbolic meaning. The retributive approach also suggests a way to seek racial progress more broadly. Many of the attitudes that whites (and others) bring to racial issues revolve around concepts of responsibility, individualism, and just deserts, such as the belief that society is open to progress only if African Americans and other minorities take greater responsibility for themselves. Responsibility and just deserts can work in the other direction, however. Society can have a responsibility (government can have responsibility) by the same logic of just deserts that often works against blacks. Our challenge is to ensure that these considerations receive fair attention in our thinking about race and racial issues.

CHAPTER 5

A Panoply of Preferences

As a whole, the legacy of the civil rights movement is ironclad and uncontested. If any part of it remains at stake, it is affirmative action. A triumph of New Deal liberalism to some and "racial engineering of a new and radical sort" to others (Thernstrom and Thernstrom 1997, 172), affirmative action simultaneously represents a noble experiment in government's ability to bring about social change and a bitter-tasting retreat from, or at least postponement of, Martin Luther King Jr.'s dream of a society where people would not be judged by the color of their skin. In few other domains do race-related aspirations, interests, and ideals—for both blacks and whites—mix as richly, or as uneasily.

The term *affirmative action* traces its origins to an executive order signed by John F. Kennedy in 1961. At the time, the only mechanisms to protect minorities in hiring practices were state-level Fair Employment Practices Commissions. Vestiges of antidiscrimination efforts from World War II, and meant to be temporary, the commissions were almost entirely toothless in their ability to integrate workplaces. They could mandate arbitration in specific cases of overt discrimination but could do little to counter the common protest of employers accused of discrimination: that blacks were not deliberately being excluded but that racially homogeneous workplaces were a by-product of the tendency to find workers through informal (but closed) kin, neighborhood, and church networks. Civil rights organizations like the National Association for the Advancement of Colored People (NAACP) and the Congress of Racial Equality (CORE) were becoming increasingly well organized and assertive. They initiated boycotts and picket lines to combat discriminatory hiring in cities like Philadelphia and Detroit. Facing such pressure but legislatively hamstrung by southern conservatives in Congress,

Kennedy sought to use executive power to bring about some change. Executive Order 10925 pushed against passive obstructionism and tokenism by directing federal agencies to "take affirmative action to ensure that applicants are employed, and that employees are treated during employment, without regard to their race, creed, color, or national origin" (Sugrue 1998).

Though the shift may seem small, its significance was monumental as it marked an expansion of the civil rights project from a focus on blacks' negative rights—their right not to be actively discriminated against, for instance—to positive rights such as the right to achieve their aspirations and potential. It moreover codified government as an agent to secure these rights.

The expansion could not come without alienating some constituencies. Unions, for instance, resented the scrutiny of hiring practices and the prospect that nepotistic hiring networks would be broken up. One union official vented, "The established and well-earned rights of white people are being imperiled in the fight of Negro leadership against unions," and the first charges of "discrimination against white persons" surfaced (Evans 1963, quoted in Sugrue 1998, 894). The consternation would reverberate, creating fault lines, some surprising, in existing political coalitions. One memorable example comes from Richard Nixon. As president, Nixon evinced notable support of civil rights, appointing civil rights sympathizers George Shultz and Arthur Fletcher as secretary and assistant secretary of labor. His endorsement for what became known as the Philadelphia Plan—a requirement that construction firms bidding for government contracts submit targets for "minority manpower utilization"—was probably genuine and not purely strategic. Nonetheless, it is easy to imagine him deriving some satisfaction from the rift such actions opened up between two Democratic constituencies: labor unions and blacks (Sugrue 2004). In this episode and similar ones, affirmative action has been blamed for the fragmentation of an interracial left-wing political coalition that supported the New Deal (Glazer 1983).

Of course, the debate over preferences continues today, although its grounds have shifted somewhat. Arguments on both sides of the issue have evolved. Although conservatives opposed the principle of race neutrality when its application meant that European whites could not favor members of their own ethnic group (Sugrue 2004), they now took up the mantle of race neutrality. Proponents, for their part, now rarely justify racial preferences as a direct response to present or past discrimination.[1] More often, they point to broad benefits of diversity or the need for minorities to reach a critical mass in a particular place to feel comfortable. And racial preferences in colleges and universities have emerged as a focus.

Putting aside disagreements over the principled rationales for and against affirmative action, its empirical consequences are also hotly debated. To sample but a small part of the relevant literature, the idea that racial preferences do in fact deliver their promised benefit gained some impressive authority and imprimatur in *The Shape of the River* (2000), a book by William Bowen and Derek Bok, the former presidents of Princeton and Harvard, respectively. Bowen and Bok trace the life paths of 45,000 college students of different races and conclude that students admitted to college with lower qualifications succeed both academically and in their careers. However, some criticize the way Bowen and Bok conduct their analysis and maintain that racial preferences, as applied, have pernicious effects. Richard Sander, Stuart Taylor, and Thomas Sowell, for instance, are among those who argue that preferences lead to an overall "shifting" and "mismatch" effect. Because affirmative action policies cause racial minorities to be admitted to more competitive institutions than would be the case without preferences, their academic performance might tend to cluster in the bottom of their respective institutions, resulting in frustration, social isolation, lower graduation rates, and less impressive credentials (in terms of GPA and so forth) when it comes to apply to jobs and graduate programs (Sander and Taylor 2012; Sowell 2005). Others suggest that racial preferences ultimately discourage minorities from pursuing majors in science, technology, engineering, and math, opting instead for easier majors (U.S. Commission on Civil Rights 2010; Arcidiacono, Aucejo, and Spenner 2011).

We approach this complex and difficult issue as public opinion researchers. The philosophical and empirical debates should and will continue. Whatever solution they identify as proper, however, is likely to be short-lived if a wave of opinion pushes against it, and affirmative action policies are notoriously unpopular. Bans have appeared on the ballot in five states between 1996 and 2008, winning majority support in four of the five elections (California, Washington, Michigan, and Nebraska). The average level of support for these bans was 57 percent. Only in Colorado did an affirmative action ban go down to defeat and there only by the smallest of margins (sharing the ballot with the 2008 presidential race, with candidate Obama generating liberal enthusiasm).[2]

From our point of view, it is evident that affirmative action is a quintessential group conflict issue. The resources that are at stake—seats in a
university—are finite, valuable, and critical to the futures of those who receive them. As Thomas and Mary Edsall put it, affirmative action created
"zero sum solutions in which the gains of one group were losses for the other"
(1991, 124). While much has been written about how hostile attitudes toward affirmative action represent the persistence of prejudice in contemporary society or an attachment to the principle of race neutrality,[3] public
disapproval of preferences also affirms what we expect given the premises of
group conflict theory.

How much of white opposition is driven by group conflict impulses?
Whatever the answer, could it be otherwise? There is reason to believe so.
Context clearly matters in how people respond to many issues, and the public opinion literature on affirmative action supports the contention of James
H. Kuklinski and colleagues (1997, 402) that attitudes toward affirmative
action "are not unyielding and inalterably fixed" but rather sensitive to other
considerations. For instance, David A. Harrison and colleagues (2006), in a
meta-analysis of 106 studies of affirmative action in employment, show that
support for affirmative action is bolstered when respondents are asked about
it in the context of the specific discrimination that affirmative action is compensating for (see also Kuklinski et al. 1997; Stoker 2001). They also find that
the argument that preferences provide important diversity to the whole has
some positive influence on affirmative action opinion (see also Richardson
2005). This is what one might expect given a perspective based in group conflict theory, as in both cases the issue is framed in such a way as to detach
black and Hispanic gains from white or Asian losses.

The next two chapters apply our approach, which should now be familiar, to this thorny issue of affirmative action. We call attention to different
ways of thinking about the issue and examine whether group conflict impulses appear to recede. As is evident in the discussion above, affirmative action is rich with crosscutting considerations of fairness and evenhandedness,
all of which carry some legitimacy and might be efficacious in changing
whites' views on the issue. In this chapter, we investigate how whites' thinking about affirmative action changes when they consider racial preferences
as just one of many preferences that college admissions officers consider.
Chapter 6 focuses a spotlight on race neutrality, a principle central to thinking about race-oriented policies that works somewhat differently in the case
of racial preferences. As we shall see, whites' opposition to racial preferences

is hardly preordained. There is room for persuasion and change even on this most difficult of issues.

Building an Ark

The starting point of our investigation is the observation that public ignorance about the multifaceted nature of the college admissions process is widespread. For one thing, in the absence of much information, many individuals tend to overestimate the impact on their own group (Crosby and Cordova 1996). In his study of selective college admissions, Thomas J. Kane (1998) calculates that the acceptance rates of whites and Asians would grow only one to two percentage points if every black and Hispanic student gave up their seat in the class, which of course assumes that none of them are admissible without an admissions preference, clearly a faulty assumption.[4] While it is not clear what people think whites/Asians are losing because of affirmative action, it is likely that they imagine that it is larger than one or two percentage points, given that most people have terrible census knowledge and systematically and grossly overestimate the percentage of minorities in the population (Highton and Wolfinger 1992; Nadeau, Niemi, and Levine 1993).

Even more important, ignorance about university admissions practices means that individuals are not likely to understand preferences in the context of the many preferences that operate in the admissions domain. The admissions process is actually loaded with preferences that go well beyond racial preferences. In order to create a diverse class that will be part of the educative environment; in order to help the university fulfill its role as an engine of social progress and change; and in order to populate classes throughout the curriculum, sports teams, and research laboratories, admissions offices offer advantages to many different kinds of students. As the dean of university administrators, Harvard's Henry Rosovsky, writes (1990, 63), "[Admissions is] an exercise in social engineering, involving high school grades, essays, interviews, recommendations from teachers, and above all a general vision concerning the composition of an ideal freshman class. That ideal is most easily defined as an optimum degree of diversity—hence my allusion to Noah's Ark—within a framework of academic excellence." By bringing these other preferences to light and discussing racial preferences in the context of all those that guide admissions decisions, perhaps there is an opportunity to get people to look at them a little bit differently and thus offer a different opinion.

Most discussions of affirmative action encourage people to think of a pie with one really large piece for whites and perhaps Asians, and one smaller, but still too big, piece for blacks and Hispanics. We suggest an alternative frame also premised upon a fixed pie, but one that is cut into very small slices allocated to all kinds of groups. In such a context, competition between whites and blacks is deemphasized. More pie for blacks does not lead the mind inexorably to think about less pie for whites, or vice versa. All different kinds of groups have legitimate claim to a piece of the pie, and this makes it more difficult to deny legitimacy to the claim of racial minorities. What is more, we argue that this frame changes how one thinks about calls to banish racial preferences from the process. Can you take away preferences for racial minorities and leave all other kinds of preferences intact? The hypothesis here is that this new frame (activated by bringing new information to people) plucks the issue from a group conflict frame and puts it into a "carved-up pie" frame. This, in and of itself, should foster more sympathetic ways of looking at affirmative action.

To test these ideas, we conducted some survey experiments in Michigan in 2006 and 2007. Michigan has been ground zero for the debate on preferences. The state's flagship university, the University of Michigan, had its admissions policies challenged in a set of cases that proceeded through the federal court system and allowed the justices to formulate the parameters for preferences in state institutions. In response to the Court's decisions and the university's claim of victory for its preferences practices, anti–affirmative action groups mobilized to present the issue as a referendum. It was during and after that political battle that we conducted our experiments to measure the impact of a carved-up-pie frame on attitudes toward preferences.

The Michigan ballot initiative was in November 2006. Our experiments were placed on three State of the State Surveys conducted out of Michigan State University. These surveys were in the field between August and October 2006, February and April 2007, and October and November 2007.[5]

Affirmative Action in Michigan

In 2003, the Supreme Court, in *Grutter v. Bollinger* and *Gratz v. Bollinger*, replaced the twenty-five-year-old ruling on affirmative action made in the famous *Bakke* decision. *Grutter* and *Gratz*, both cases that emerged from challenges to admissions policies at the University of Michigan, essentially established a split decision on affirmative action. In the latter decision, the court found that the university's undergraduate admissions policies, which rigidly included race and ethnicity in a mathematical admissions formula, were unconstitutional. But in the former case, Justice Sandra Day O'Connor gave the university law school's policy "a limited reprieve" according to a conservative critic of the decision (Levey 2003, B11). She and her colleagues in the majority ruled that the law school's admissions assessments were more qualitative and less mechanical, allowed for a less rigid (and thus acceptable) use of race in admissions decisions, and included many different aspects of diversity, not just race and ethnicity.

More important, Justice O'Connor's decision offered justification for affirmative action beyond its value to members of racial minority groups. Justice O'Connor was persuaded by amicus briefs from a collection of former military generals, from private industry, and from many institutions of higher learning. These briefs made the case that diversity was an important value to their institutions and that affirmative action in higher education was critical to achieving that diversity. In the military, a diverse officer corps is essential to a well-functioning operation, the generals argued, particularly given the diversity found in the enlisted ranks. Pointing to the affirmative action policies in place at the service academies, they encouraged the justices to think differently about preferences, and their arguments were quite influential with the justices (Toobin 2007, 256). Likewise, over sixty major corporations filed briefs supporting the university, including Michigan-based General Motors, Dow Chemical, and Daimler Chrysler (Parker 2003). Their arguments about the benefits of affirmative action to their businesses were clearly influential with the justices in general and Justice O'Connor in particular (Greenhouse 2003). Not surprisingly, many colleges and universities rallied to the support of the University of Michigan and contributed briefs to the judicial record. All of these arguments were fully incorporated into Justice O'Connor's opinion. As she wrote:

> The Law School's claim is further bolstered by numerous expert studies and reports showing that such diversity promotes learning outcomes and better prepares students for an increasingly diverse workforce, for society, and for the legal profession. Major American businesses have made clear that the skills needed in today's increasingly global

marketplace can only be developed through exposure to widely diverse people, cultures, ideas, and viewpoints. High-ranking retired officers and civilian military leaders assert that a highly qualified, racially diverse officer corps is essential to national security. Moreover, because universities, and in particular, law schools, represent the training ground for a large number of the Nation's leaders, *Sweatt* v. *Painter*, 339 U.S. 629, 634, the path to leadership must be visibly open to talented and qualified individuals of every race and ethnicity. Thus, the Law School has a compelling interest in attaining a diverse student body. (*Grutter v. Bollinger*, 539 U.S. 306 [2003])

In making this argument, Justice O'Connor was building upon logic that Justice Lewis Powell first articulated in his *Bakke* decision, where he was the lone proponent of this view. It became a central point of her opinion. Essentially, in the university, diversity provides all students exposure to difference. There is much learning and preparation for the future contained in that exposure.

The opinion was not a ringing endorsement of university preferences. It is important to note that Justice O'Connor also placed a time limitation on the practice of affirmative action, declaring that in twenty-five years, the policy should no longer be necessary. There was no science to this deadline—it came from an observation that a quarter century had passed since *Bakke* (Toobin 2007, 262–263)—and it is certainly not enforceable. But it is important because this limitation demonstrated her skepticism of race-based preferential treatment. Despite this less positive gloss that she put on the decision, the University of Michigan declared victory in the case. Although it was a mixed decision, it did allow the university and its peers to continue to consider diversity in admissions decisions. If Michigan's undergraduate admissions process was invalidated in the *Gratz* case, some modest alterations in how preferences are implemented would allow racial preferences to continue in the undergraduate admissions process.

The story in Michigan does not end there, however. The Court's decisions led activists, including Jennifer Gratz, the plaintiff in one of the court cases, to challenge affirmative action in the public sphere through a ballot initiative. After a vigorous campaign, the 2006 proposition, which banned both race- and gender-based preferences in state hiring, contracting, and education decisions, garnered 58 percent of the vote. Although in the immediate wake of the vote, defiant University of Michigan president Mary Sue Coleman vowed to challenge the outcome (Slevin 2006), the government and the state universities have adjusted their practices to accommodate the law. The University of Michigan itself has kept its racial and ethnic diversity intact with extraordinary recruitment efforts and by giving preferences to geographical areas densely populated by minorities.

Preferences in College Admissions

In fact, black and Hispanic students do receive preferences in admissions at elite private institutions and state universities alike. Though state universities are constrained by the Supreme Court's decisions in their practice of affirmative action, even these university systems have devised alternative ways to admit and enroll a more diverse class.

How large is this preference and how does it stack up against other advantages that exist in admissions systems? Thomas Espenshade and colleagues provide a handle on this question in their analysis of more than 100,000 admissions decisions at ten elite colleges and universities (Espenshade, Chung, and Walling 2004). The data they analyze are not entirely current, coming from the 1980s, 1993, and 1997. Because racial preferences have likely decreased since those years (Grodsky and Kalogrides 2008), the results may overstate the extent of racial preferences. Still, they provide some perspective on how racial preferences compare to other preferences that exist.

Espenshade and colleagues conduct their analysis by estimating a logistical regression, which is a statistical tool that predicts how different features (e.g., race) contribute to the odds of occurrence of an event (e.g., gaining admission to a university). Because the standard output of a logistical regression is somewhat difficult to interpret—it produces odds ratios, which are not intuitive for most people—we use their results to conduct a simple simulation that predicts the chances that various imaginary students would gain admission to a hypothetical selective university. The simulation is shown in Table 5.1, which depicts the chances of admission for these imaginary students.[6] (Note that the data for this analysis come from a time when the maximum possible SAT score was 1600.)

Preferences for blacks and Hispanics are clearly evident. Within each SAT score stratum, a black or Hispanic applicant's chances of admission are higher than a comparable white applicant. Sometimes they are much higher. For the middle SAT strata, for instance, blacks are as much as three times

Table 5.1. Probability of Admission at Hypothetical Selective University

	White	White legacy	White athlete	Black	Hispanic	Asian
SAT score (maximum 1600)						
<1000	1%	3%	4%	5%	3%	1%
1050	3	10	13	16	11	2
1150	9	23	28	34	26	6
1250	16	36	44	50	40	12
1350	26	52	59	66	56	20
1450	43	70	76	80	73	35
1550	66	85	89	91	88	58

Notes: Simulation based on Table 2, Model 7 of Espenshade et al. (2004). We begin by positing a baseline white applicant who has an SAT score of 1250 and a 16 percent chance of admission (which captures the idea of a selective university). We then use the regression results to simulate what the chance of admission would be for other hypothetical applicants. Controls for sex and citizenship status were included in the original model.

more likely to gain admission than a comparable white applicant, with a slightly lower, but still substantial, preference going to Hispanics. Asians, on the other hand, exhibit a moderate disadvantage relative to whites. But how substantial are these preferences relative to other ones?

Many private universities bestow admissions benefits on so-called legacy applicants, children of school alumni. It is thought that such preferences assist the financial development of the school and contribute to its sense of tradition and culture. The analysis of Espenshade and colleagues finds the legacy advantage also to be substantial. As can be seen in Table 5.1, being a legacy applicant is almost as advantageous as being Hispanic.

Another admissions advantage is bestowed on students who have athletic talents identified by coaches. It is thought that, by supporting sports teams, student athletes contribute to the school's sense of community. And, of course, there are some universities where sports like football and basketball are a significant source of revenue. How big an admissions advantage do student athletes enjoy? As Table 5.1 shows, being an athlete is even more advantageous than being Hispanic.

There are other preferences that we cannot analyze. Many universities offer tuition benefits for the children of staff and faculty. Given the all-or-nothing nature of the benefit, this policy puts enormous pressure on the admissions office to admit these students. From our experience, while many of these applicants are strong, there is a gap between the university-affiliated admitted student and all other students, which illustrates the existence of yet another preference practiced by admissions, one of importance to the morale of the faculty and staff at the university. Likewise, geography can play a role in admissions decisions. Because applicant pools are often tilted toward the local region and states that are notorious "student exporters" (such as New Jersey and Connecticut), and because the admissions office sees value in having some geographic diversity in the class, some applicants—those from Middle America, for instance—are often advantaged over others.

Finally, recent years have seen the patterns with respect to gender reverse in a notable way. Girls now significantly outperform boys in high school academics. Inductees in the National Honor Society are 64 percent female. As of 2005, the average high school grade point average for girls is 3.09 but only 2.86 for boys (Whitmire 2010, 211). Even the ambition of girls is more apparent. Among high school sophomores, girls are more likely than boys to indicate that they planned to attend college, 84 percent versus 75 percent, and their high school choices reflect this, with 54 percent of girls and 48 percent of boys enrolled in college prep curricula (National Center for Education Statistics 2006). The result of both ambition and performance is that college applicant pools are more heavily female, with two-thirds of universities reporting more female applicants than male (Britz 2006). If universities were to distribute admissions so that they reflected the pool, their classes would be tilted in problematic ways.[7] Although females used to receive admissions preference, admissions offices now are more likely to practice affirmative action for male students, taking less accomplished boys over more accomplished girls at the margins. As the dean of admissions at Kenyon College writes, "The fat acceptance envelope is simply more elusive for today's accomplished young women" (Britz 2006). This change is a testament, if a bittersweet one, to the academic success of women.[8]

One final preference of note is that given to those students who come from families capable of paying the bill. Financial aid is a scarce resource and most universities are not need blind. A need-blind process is one where the admissions office makes all admissions decisions without taking into consideration the ability to pay. The financial aid office then pays for the outcome of that process, whatever it may be. Only 18 percent of private universities in the country report that they are both need blind in process and committed to addressing the full financial need of their admitted students (Jaschik 2008). Universities that are not need blind thus practice preferences for students who can pay and in so doing avoid the risk of an unpredictable outcome that can overwhelm the resources allocated to financial aid. Tufts University, for instance, is committed to meeting the full need of all of its students, but the admissions process is not need blind.[9] The admissions office settles on a tentative admitted class. That class is "priced" by the financial aid director. The office then shuffles students around so that some "full-pay" students are admitted while others with significant need are taken out of the admitted pool. This only happens on the margin, but it does lead to some changes. In March 2009, with ten days to go before admissions decisions were released, 60 percent of the accepted students had requested financial aid. To accommodate the finite financial aid resources, the admissions office pulled back about two hundred admitted students and added two hundred others, so that only 55 percent of accepted students would request financial aid.[10] In the entirety of the pool, these numbers are quite small, but the mechanics of the process and the outcome illustrates how this preference operates to the benefit of some and the disadvantage of others.

The college admissions process is thus one in which myriad preferences apply. As admissions offices seek diverse classes ("diverse" defined in many different ways); as they face applications from the children of alumni, faculty, and staff; as they try to balance gender and geography; as they try to maximize their financial aid budgets, some students have advantages over others. Though crosscutting advantages are often at play—students are advantaged on some dimensions and not others—there are winners and losers.[11] This, of course, is not the perception of the admissions process that most people have when they think about college preferences.

The Impact of Information

What if people are asked to think about racial preferences in the context of all of the other preferences that exist in the system? The hypothesis driving this exercise is that information about college admissions, information that most people are not familiar with, should influence how people consider racial preferences. Such information should activate or reorient a fairness heuristic that is clearly in place when the issue concerns only race, thus neutralizing the desire to protect one's in-group.

The starting point for this exercise is a battery of questions on a 2003 *Newsweek* survey conducted as the University of Michigan affirmative

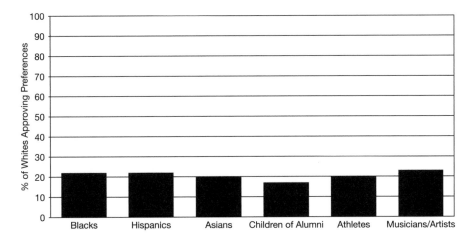

Figure 5.1. White Approval of Preferences in Admissions for Different Groups
Source: Newsweek Poll (January 18, 2003), Princeton Survey Research Associates. Percentages reported here are for non-Hispanic whites (n=768).

Question wording:

Please tell me whether you think colleges and universities should or should not give preferences in admissions for each of the following groups. [First] what about [blacks]? Should there be preferences in admissions for this group, or not?

action cases were under consideration by the Supreme Court. The unusual survey is actually premised upon the notion that preferences are widespread, and respondents are asked whether admission advantages should be granted to various groups, leading off with blacks but then extending to other racial groups (Hispanics, Asians) and various identifiable groups that often are advantaged in the selection process (children of alumni, athletes, and musicians/artists). What is clear from this survey is that preferences are unpopular across the board. Notably, there is remarkably little variation in support for preferences for different groups. The range of support actually runs between 17 and 23 percent (see Figure 5.1), but it is important to note that the format of the questions may have had something to do with this consistency. With the lead question about blacks, respondents who have rejected preferences for blacks might find it difficult, in the context of a battery of related questions, to accept preferences for other groups. That there is not more support for preferences for athletes, musicians, and artists despite the fact that there is a merit or talent basis for preferring them suggests that respondents are handcuffed by their first answer and implies that respondents do fall back on some kind of neutrality principle (see Chapter 6). Once applied to blacks, the neutrality principle appears to activate and is applied to the other groups, even to the point that the merit consideration is lost.

The *Newsweek* survey offers an interesting insight in suggesting that respondents are making race-neutral judgments. We attempt to test this with a further experiment. What if *Newsweek* asked about the groups in reverse order? If support for preferences for athletes, legacy applicants, and artists is dampened by the answer respondents have given moments earlier for blacks and Hispanics, can we boost support for racial preferences by asking first about athletes, legacy applicants, and artists? In a survey experiment conducted in Michigan, we test this possibility. In this experiment, a random half of our respondents are asked about preferences in the same order that *Newsweek* respondents were asked. The other half of respondents are asked about athletes, legacy applicants, and musicians/artists first, blacks and Hispanics second. If the hypothesis were born out, the act of approving nonracial preferences should create greater support for racial preferences, either because the former questions have added new information into the respondent's calculus or because they simply highlight a fairness standard.

Alas, the results of the experiment provide only modest support for the hypothesis (Table 5.2). The initial set of results is notably consistent with the results of the *Newsweek* survey. Despite being drawn from Michigan, the actual level of support for preferences for the various groups is very close to the national results of three years prior (looking at the results for non-Hispanic whites). Moreover, respondents in the Michigan survey rank the different preference targets just as they did in the national survey, with legacy applicants the least popular target of preferences, musicians/artists the most popular. But the predominant finding is that the question order has only a modest impact on responses to the question of racial preferences. Looking at the responses of non-Hispanic whites, support for racial preferences increases when this question is asked at the end of the battery, but only by five percentage points, a difference small enough to have arisen by chance (two-tailed $p = .11$).

While the impact of question order on attitudes toward racial preferences is quite modest, there is nonetheless some suggestion that question order is meaningful here. What is striking is that there is substantial change in support for nonracial preferences from the first treatment to the second. Support for preferences goes up significantly in all three cases, particularly for musicians and artists, when these responses are not dampened by an initial re-

Table 5.2. Question Order Only Modestly Affects Views on Preferences for Blacks and Hispanics

All respondents

	Order of questions →				
	Blacks	Hispanics	Athletes	Legacy applicants	Artists & musicians
% approve preferences	.28[a]	.27[b]	.21	.18	.26
	(447)	(452)	(461)	(450)	(457)
	Athletes	Legacy applicants	Artists & musicians	Blacks	Hispanics
% approve preferences	.28	.25	.42	.31[a]	.30[b]
	(485)	(482)	(485)	(487)	(488)

Non-Hispanic white respondents

	Order of questions →				
	Blacks	Hispanics	Athletes	Legacy applicants	Artists & musicians
% approve preferences	.19[c]	.19[d]	.15	.13	.19
	(349)	(353)	(358)	(354)	(355)
	Athletes	Legacy applicants	Artists & musicians	Blacks	Hispanics
% approve preferences	.24	.24	.39	.24[c]	.24[d]
	(376)	(375)	(375)	(377)	(377)

Source: Michigan State of the State Survey (August–October 2006).

[a] $t = -.93, p < .36$

[b] $t = -.98, p < .33$

[c] $t = 1.41, p < .16$

[d] $t = 1.62, p < .11$

Question wording:

Please tell me whether you think colleges and universities should or should not give preferences in admissions for each of the following groups. First, what about blacks? Should there be preferences in admissions for this group or not? What about [Hispanics/athletes/children of alumni/musicians and artists]? Should there be preferences in admissions for this group or not?

Please tell me whether you think colleges and universities should or should not give preferences in admissions for each of the following groups? First, what about athletes? Should there be preferences in admissions for this group or not? What about [children of alumni/musicians and artists/blacks/Hispanics]? Should there be preferences in admissions for this group or not?

sponse to a question of racial preferences. Among non-Hispanic whites, support for an admissions advantage for musicians/artists goes up twenty percentage points, while support for athletes and legacies jumps ten percentage points when these preferences are asked about prior to racial preferences.[12]

This question-wording experiment is actually rather subtle, relying upon respondents to make a connection between racial and nonracial preferences when this connection is not explicit in the question. Before rejecting the hypothesis altogether, and armed with a sense from the previous results that more information might establish a new definition of fairness, we have constructed another, less subtle test. In this experiment, conducted on a series of consecutive Michigan State of the State Surveys, respondents are randomly asked one of several questions about their attitude toward preferences.[13] The responses from these different questions are then compared to the responses reported in Table 5.2 (where blacks/Hispanic preferences are asked about first, parallel to the question used in the original *Newsweek* survey): "Please tell me whether you think colleges and universities should or should not give preferences in admissions for each of the following groups. First, what about Blacks/Hispanics? Should there be preferences in admissions for this group or not?"[14] Respondents are randomly distributed into a series of variations on the question and are asked their position on preferences in the context of some other preference. Athletes, legacy applicants, and artists/musicians are grouped together in one of these treatments: "Colleges and universities give admissions preferences to many groups of students, such as athletes, children of alumni, and artists and musicians. Should there also be preferences in admissions for blacks and Hispanics?" Other treatments ask about racial preferences in the context of preferences for scientists and leaders, men, and full-pay students. Each of these questions tells the respondent about the preference and the reason for the preference, a consideration that might also apply to students of color, before asking about racial preferences:

> In promoting certain societal goals, colleges and universities give admissions preferences to many groups of students, such as students interested in science and technology, and students with leadership qualities. Should there also be preferences in admissions for blacks and Hispanics?

> In constructing a balanced student body, colleges and universities give admissions preferences to many groups of students, including

male students. Should there also be preferences in admissions for blacks and Hispanics?

Colleges and universities give admissions preferences to many groups of students, such as those from families that can afford to pay full tuition. Should there also be preferences in admissions for blacks and Hispanics?

In Table 5.3, we provide the results from these experiments. Perhaps because there is additional information provided in the question, or perhaps because the link between preferences for other groups and racial preferences is completely explicit, the different wordings clearly have a pronounced effect. In each case, the context provided in the question appears to matter. Respondents in each of the treatments are more likely than respondents in the contextless question to approve of racial preferences. Notably, there is a fair amount of variation in the impact of the different treatments. In every case, the inclusion of additional information about which groups receive admissions preferences has some impact on support for racial preferences; in some cases, the difference is dramatic. In the context of full-pay students, support for racial preferences almost doubles among non-Hispanic whites from the baseline of 22 percent to 43 percent. Support for racial preferences goes up to 41 percent when non-Hispanic whites are told about preferences for athletes, legacy applicants, and artists/musicians. This is particularly remarkable when compared with the impact of the implicit treatment, which had such a modest effect. Clearly, the connections need to be drawn boldly in order to have an impact on responses.

As two of the questions include a rationale for the preferences and two do not, one possibility is that the rationales, not the contextual information about the preferences, are moving opinions. The findings are not consistent with this hypothesis, however. The two questions with brief rationales—"constructing a balanced student body" (in preferring men to women) and "promoting certain societal goals" (in preferring scientists and leaders)—have lower levels of support than the two questions where the rationale is not embedded in the question. The fact that the information about preferences for scientists and leaders generates the least support for racial preferences of the four alternatives suggests that the question is tapping into considerations of merit, though we would note that the question does not say whether the applicants are good scientists, only interested scientists.

Table 5.3. Informing Respondents About Other Preferences Leads to Greater
Support for Black/Hispanic Preferences (Mean Scores)

Support for Black / Hispanic Preferences

		In the context of support for . . .			
	Baseline	*Athletes, legacy applicants, artists, musicians*	*Scientists and leaders*	*Men*	*Full-pay students*
All respondents	.30	.49	.35	.40	.51
	(946)	(591)	(292)	(300)	(313)
t	—	7.4***	1.6	2.8***	6.6***
Non-Hispanic whites	.22	.41	.28	.34	.43
	(729)	(449)	(230)	(220)	(232)
t	—	7.1***	1.8*	3.6***	6.4***
		$* p < .10$	$** p < .05$	$*** p < .01$	

Source: Michigan State of the State Survey (August–October 2006, February–April 2007,
October–November 2007).

Question wording:
Baseline: Please tell me whether you think colleges and universities should or should not give
preferences in admissions for each of the following groups. First, what about blacks? Should
there be preferences in admissions for this group or not? What about Hispanics? Should there be
preferences in admissions for this group or not? Respondents who approve of preferences for
blacks or Hispanics or both are counted here as approving preferences generally.

Colleges and universities give admissions preferences to many groups of students, such as
athletes, children of alumni, and artists and musicians. Should there also be preferences in
admissions for blacks and Hispanics?

In promoting certain societal goals, colleges and universities give admissions preferences to many
groups of students, such as students interested in science and technology, and students with
leadership qualities. Should there also be preferences in admissions for blacks and Hispanics?

In constructing a balanced student body, colleges and universities give admissions preferences
to many groups of students, including male students. Should there also be preferences in
admissions for blacks and Hispanics?

Colleges and universities give admissions preferences to many groups of students, such as those
from families that can afford to pay full tuition. Should there also be preferences in admissions
for blacks and Hispanics?

Finally, it is worth noting that including information about nonracial
preferences in the survey questions clearly has some potential to change the
orientation of non-Hispanic whites to the question of racial preferences, but
this is also true of nonwhites. Looking at the effect of the experiment on
all respondents, regardless of race, shows that majority support for racial

preferences can be generated in the most persuasive context, breaking a high and important threshold.

Taking Away Some Preferences, Not Others

Up to this point, all of the questions we have used have been about whether racial preferences are acceptable, and this is the predominant way that studies of public attitudes ask about preferences. Yet all of the real-world political, judicial, and electoral tests of the preference issue have been questions of whether racial preferences should be jettisoned. With this in mind, what if the experimental questions used thus far are reframed to reflect the way that legislators, judges, and voters face the issue? Does this reframing make the additional information about nonracial preferences more potent? It very well could, given that respondents would then be asked about abandoning racial preferences while leaving these other preferences in place. This, of course, is exactly what happens when racial preferences are tossed out.

To test this hypothesis, we compare responses to the question of racial preferences in the context of other preferences ("Colleges and universities give admissions preferences to many groups of students, such as athletes, children of alumni, and artists and musicians. Should there also be preferences in admissions for blacks and Hispanics?") with responses to a parallel question that frames the issue as taking away preferences ("Colleges and universities give admissions preferences to many groups of students, such as athletes, children of alumni, and artists and musicians. Is it right for preferences in admissions for blacks and Hispanics to be taken away?").

The difference in responses to these two questions is huge and statistically significant (Table 5.4). While almost half of all respondents agree that there should be preferences for blacks and Hispanics in college admissions (as there are for other groups), three-quarters of all respondents reject the idea that racial preferences should be taken away while the other preferences remain in place. Even among non-Hispanic whites, the three-quarters threshold is just about met. It is hard to imagine a more powerful evocation of support for racial preferences.

There is one alternative explanation for the power of the frame that should be raised before settling on the conclusion that the take-away frame is responsible for the persuasiveness of the question. While the question does not employ a double negative, the take-away frame does require an extra

Table 5.4. Respondents are Loath to Take Away Preferences (Mean Scores)

	Should there be preferences for blacks, Hispanics?	Should preferences be taken away?
All respondents	.49	.76
	(591)	(302)
t	—	8.1***
Non-Hispanic whites	.41	.72
	(449)	(226)
t	—	8.0***
	* $p < .10$ ** $p < .05$	*** $p < .01$

Source: Michigan State of the State Survey (February–April 2007, October–November 2007).

Question wording:

Preferences for? Colleges and universities give admissions preferences to many groups of students, such as athletes, children of alumni, and artists and musicians. Should there also be preferences in admissions for blacks and Hispanics?

Take preferences away? Colleges and universities give admissions preferences to many groups of students, such as athletes, children of alumni, and artists and musicians. Is it right for preferences in admissions for blacks and Hispanics to be taken away? (Figure in table represents those *disagreeing* with this question.)

cognitive step that the original question does not (agreement with the statement means rejecting preferences and vice versa). Could the take-away wording be confusing people and thus heightening support for preferences? One way to evaluate this question is to break down the sample by level of education. If the wording is confusing, one might expect less educated respondents to be more likely to agree with the statement and appear to react to the frame. In fact, the frame works across all education subgroups and has about the same impact on each group. Within each education subgroup, the comparison of the two frames reaches statistical significance. Better-educated respondents are more supportive of preferences in response to both frames, but there is no indication that the take-away frame is confusing less educated respondents in a way that is shaping the results.

Our argument is that the take-away frame, together with the information about other preferences at work in the system (which would continue), has persuasive power. It is not clear, however, if the take-away frame is the primary influence here, or if it is a catalyst that gives the political information even more potency. One might turn to Prospect Theory, which asserts that framing

CHAPTER 6

A Spotlight on Race Neutrality

Principles are integral to the debate over racial issues. To bring down Jim Crow and to promote an integrated society, the leaders of the civil rights movement and political liberals argued for race neutrality. One of the iconic moments of the movement is Martin Luther King Jr.'s "I Have a Dream" speech, his dream, "deeply rooted in the American dream," being a day when his children would "not be judged by the color of their skin, but by the content of their character." So successful was King's speech in evoking American values, writes historian Taylor Branch (1988, 887), that it "projected him across the racial divide and planted him as a new founding father."

As we describe in the previous chapter, as the civil rights movement evolved "from protest to politics" (Tate 1993), progressives began advocating affirmative action as a way to overcome token integration and compensate for institutional practices that made it difficult for blacks to compete with whites for jobs, education, and other resources (Sugrue 1998). Although it was a landmark step and likely necessary, the embrace of affirmative action as a vehicle for social change detached the civil rights movement from its race-neutral moorings. The left did not surrender race neutrality completely to the right; efforts to end discrimination and racial profiling were still justified by race neutrality. But on many other racial issues of the day, black and minority leaders advocated and continue to advocate policies that are not race neutral.

Conservatives, who had generally opposed racial change and the civil rights movement, responded accordingly. In the years following the civil rights movement, they incorporated race neutrality into their own conceptualizations of problems and solutions and into their rhetoric, particularly in their opposition to affirmative action. Indeed, once the civil rights movement was over, they boldly laid claim to its legacy. How striking it was to hear Newt Gingrich, at a meeting of political scientists, remark that the only mistake of the modern conservative movement has been its opposition to the civil rights movement, a movement whose aims he now wholly embraced (American Political Science Association Plenary Session 2000). And this makes sense, for the conservative rejection of affirmative action, racial districting, and many other racial policies is rooted in a race-neutral logic. In its most virtuous form, the conservative argument is not about whites losing valuable opportunities to blacks. Rather it is about rewarding merit and talent in a color-blind fashion, a point much in line with a general conservative attachment to individualism, competition, and just deserts.

If racial preferences violate American values and might even hurt blacks (see the claims referenced in the beginning of the previous chapter), is the alternative simply to move to a system of unfettered competition? The argument of some anti–affirmative action leaders, at least with regard to education policy, has become more benign. We should aim to help people who are disadvantaged, they argue, but disadvantage must be defined without reference to race. After 1994, Speaker Gingrich put the Republican position on affirmative action this way. His party was interested in finding ways to help people "who are financially and culturally deprived," but it opposed what he called "genetically based patterns or grievance-based patterns" of assistance (Merida 1995, A09). After 2000, the Bush Administration proposed class-based solutions they labeled "affirmative access," a system by which large numbers of blacks and Hispanics are incidentally admitted to universities by virtue of policies promoting social-class diversity. Basing college admissions on class rank and bringing in students from a diversity of high schools, for instance, accomplishes some sense of diversity without relying upon race per se.

The dialogue between liberals and conservatives over racial policy sets the context within which ordinary Americans understand and think about these issues. Not surprisingly, given how valuable the concept seems to be for politicians, race neutrality does appear to resonate with ordinary Americans. As Donald Kinder and Lynn Sanders (1996) show, race neutral programs and policies are popular with both blacks and whites, even if they can be characterized as more costly and thus infringing on self-interest (184). This general stance is also evident in public attitudes toward class-based affirmative action. Polls taken in 2003 in the wake of the Supreme Court's

University of Michigan affirmative action cases (discussed in Chapter 5) show that the public is very much in favor of class-based university preferences; roughly two-thirds of whites and about 70 percent of blacks and other minorities support class-based affirmative action (Barrett 2003; Savage 2003). Clearly, class-based affirmative action is more popular than affirmative action as it is usually conceived.

This chapter examines the nexus of race neutrality and group conflict. We focus on two sets of questions. First, how do these two concepts interact? As noted above, there are some issues where the logic of race neutrality compels outcomes favorable to blacks and other minorities (antidiscrimination policies; anti–racial profiling policies) and others where it urges policies that work against the interests of blacks and other minorities (affirmative action and racial districting). Do group conflict impulses have a harder time getting a foothold on issues where race neutrality benefits minority interests? Is group conflict more pronounced on issues where race neutrality benefits white interests?

The second set of questions focuses on support for class-based (rather than race-based) college admissions preferences. Class-based policies are more popular, putatively because they are consonant with the principle of race neutrality, and in our view, because they are less likely to activate competition-based racial hostility. Who is won over by the race-neutral alternative of class-based preferences? Is it effective even among people who have registered opposition to race-focused affirmative action? Are conservatives especially likely to respond because the class-based alternative is especially congruent with individualistic values? Finally, is the principle of race neutrality adhered to irrespective of self-interest?

We take on these two sets of questions using question-wording experiments conducted in New Jersey and California in 1999 and 2000. We placed the experiments on statewide telephone surveys conducted by the *Newark Star-Ledger*/Eagleton-Rutgers Poll of New Jersey and the California Field Poll.[1] Both survey organizations provided large representative samples of their state populations without screening for likely voters. To preview our findings, the results show that race neutrality does resonate with whites in a genuine and authentic way; the principle is more than just talk. Martin Luther King Jr. and the leaders of the civil rights movement were right to tailor their aspirations, strategy, and public message to the principle of race neutrality. As we think about political solutions to racial problems, we attempt to show that this legacy of the movement, the linkage of racial progress to race neutrality, still applies. There are race-neutral approaches to these issues that can generate sincere white support.

Race on the New Jersey Turnpike

In March 1999, the superintendent of the New Jersey state troopers, Colonel Carl Williams, offered a glimpse of his views. For months, he had forcefully rejected a charge coming from minority communities that his department practiced racial profiling. The previous April, state police patrolling the New Jersey Turnpike had pulled over a van containing four minority men. The stop went awry and police fired eleven shots at the van, injuring three of the men inside, two seriously. The incident generated a great deal of anger in minority communities as it dramatically highlighted the greater police scrutiny that black and Hispanic drivers face. When the officers involved were charged with attempted murder, Williams vigorously denied that his state police utilized profiling, stating that "racial profiling, or any form of discrimination for that matter, is not and will not be tolerated" (Allen and Singleton 1998, 11). His words did not stop the Reverend Al Sharpton and six hundred of his followers from staging a protest at the site of the shooting, an event that stopped traffic on the turnpike for nearly an hour.

The following February, a Hispanic state trooper charged that he had been harassed by his colleagues, instructed to practice profiling by his supervisors and partners, and discriminated against by his superiors for complaining. When he filed a lawsuit in federal court with the explosive racial profiling charge, Williams again defended his organization with practiced words: "racial profiling—or any form of discrimination for that matter—is not, and will not be, tolerated" (Preston 1999, B5). Yet the issue continued to ferment as groups like the Black Ministers Council of New Jersey, Black Cops Against Police Brutality, and the American Civil Liberties Union led a campaign against profiling.

A few weeks later, in a candid moment during an interview with a Newark reporter, Williams expanded upon his previous comments on the issue. He started with his firm position: "As far as racial profiling is concerned, that is absolutely not right. It never has been condoned in the State Police and it never will be condoned in the State Police." But he appeared to argue that there was a basis to discriminatory traffic enforcement on the turnpike, noting that the illegal drug trade had a racial component. As he told a reporter, "Today with this drug problem, the drug problem is cocaine or marijuana. It is most likely a minority group that's involved with that. They aren't going to ask some Irishman to be a part of their gang because they don't trust them. . . . If you're looking at the methamphetamine market, that seems to be controlled by motorcycle gangs, which are basically predominantly white. If you're looking at heroin and stuff like that, your involvement there is more or less Jamaicans" (McGraw 1999, A01). He reportedly added, "Two weeks ago, the president of the United States went to Mexico to talk to the president of Mexico about drugs. He didn't go to Ireland. He didn't go to England." Within hours of the publication of the interview, after black political leaders had staged an outraged press conference, Williams was fired by Governor Christine Todd Whitman, not for racial profiling, but for "feeding a perception of racial bias" (Zolper 1999).

The repercussions of these events in New Jersey focused attention on the issue as never before. Up and down the Eastern Seaboard, states initiated studies of racial profiling. Class action suits were filed on behalf of minority drivers. Legislation was introduced that required all traffic stops, not just arrests, to be recorded. In Congress, Representative John Conyers promised federal action along these lines as well. Even President Clinton commented upon the issue, announcing in a radio address that he was "deeply concerned" by reports of police misconduct and "racial profiling," and noting that even the perception of these problems has "shaken some communities' faith in the police who are there to protect them" (Harris 1999).

Public opinion surveys of this time are fascinating, not just because of the polling results but because of the questions that pollsters were using. Respondents were not asked their opinion of racial profiling per se. Profiling being illegal, pollsters instead asked respondents whether they believed the state police were doing a good job and whether they believed that the police actually practiced profiling. Not surprisingly, whites and minorities had dramatically different perceptions on both these questions, with whites more than three times as likely as blacks and Hispanics (73 percent versus 22 percent) to approve of the performance of the state police and blacks more than twice as likely as whites to believe that profiling was taking place (84 percent versus 39 percent; *New York Times* 1999b). Subsequent evidence strongly suggested that minorities were right on this question. Although blacks and Hispanics constituted only 13.5 percent of turnpike drivers, they represented 46 percent of drivers stopped by the state police (Cole 1999, 38) and 84 percent of the 764 arrests made by eight troopers under scrutiny for profiling (Barstow and Kocieniewski 2000). A release of documents by the state in 2000 found explicit endorsement of racial profiling, such as training materials that advised troopers to use "occupant identifiers" such as race to identify possible drug couriers, and a confidential memo that stated, "New Jersey's road troopers should necessarily be encountering and arresting a significant number of black and Hispanic criminals" (Barstow and Kocieniewski 2000).

Group Conflict and Race Neutrality

The episode in New Jersey inspires an examination of how whites' responses to group conflict vary depending on how the principle of race neutrality applies. The studies to come employ a new way to explore these dynamics: an experimental "ratcheting up" of group conflict. Our design requires a brief detour to explain its logic and background.

The predominant approach to group conflict is to study white attitudes in a variety of different settings, those where competition is necessarily heightened because blacks (and in some cases, other minorities) comprise a larger proportion of the population, and those where blacks are relatively fewer (Wright 1977; Glaser 1994; Giles and Hertz 1994; Oliver and Mendelberg 2000, to name just a few). There are some obstacles to studying group competition this way. One is endogeneity: there are other aspects of the political and social environment that might muddy a clear analysis of competitive dynamics. For instance, if close proximity between races increases quality interracial interactions at the same time that competition contributes to division between groups, then the net effects could cancel each other out.[2] Furthermore, whites who do not like blacks are free to move away, and they frequently do for this reason (Crowder and South 2008). Thus one's attitudes may affect one's environment just as one's environment may affect one's attitudes, particularly where the environment is defined by smaller boundaries like a zip code or a precinct. Finally, there are measurement issues. What is the best unit with which to measure racial environment? How can we be sure that people even recognize the racial balance in their environment? Most of these studies assume accurate perceptions of the environment. All this is to suggest that we might benefit from exploring other ways to measure the heightening of group competition and how it affects individual attitudes.

What if we could experimentally induce group conflict thinking? Results from the American National Election Study (ANES) point to a way we might do so. From 1964 to 1992, the ANES asked respondents whether they believed civil rights leaders were "trying to push too fast, are going too slowly," or are "moving at about the right speed." The question stands apart from several other race-focused questions on the instrument—such as those attempting to measure general feelings toward blacks, stereotypes, or attitudes toward specific policies—because of its close link to group conflict themes. It focuses not on feelings toward blacks as a group or stereotypes about blacks but rather what blacks are doing.

When we compare this question to other standard measures as predictors of race-related attitudes, it appears to contribute something distinct and meaningful. Consider the simple analysis in Table 6.1. Here, we take attitudes toward affirmative action (as captured on the 1992 ANES) and regress them on the standard measures of race-related attitudes—racial resentment, the black feeling thermometer, and black stereotypes—as well as the question whether "civil rights leaders are trying to push too fast." The latter question is significantly predictive of attitudes toward both affirmative action and quotas in education. A likelihood ratio test confirms that it significantly improves fit of the models ($p < .03$ for affirmative action; $p < .01$ for quotas in education). By way of contrast, the stereotyping scale does not significantly predict attitudes on these racial policies.

The apparent efficacy of the attitude captured by the black assertiveness question provides the basis for a question-wording experiment conducted in New Jersey in the year following the firing of New Jersey superintendent Carl Williams. In this experiment, which we call the Black Opinion Leader Experiment, we look at responses to two issues, affirmative action in job hiring/promotion and racial profiling. For each issue, plausible pro and con arguments are embedded in the question. The experimental manipulation comes from whether the pro argument is attributed to vaguely defined "others" or whether it explicitly comes from blacks. Thus, half of respondents heard this question: "I'd like to ask you a question on the issue of giving minorities preferences in job hirings and promotions. Some say that such preferences are wrong because they give blacks advantages they haven't earned. Others say that because of past discrimination, blacks should be given such preferences. How about you? Are you for or against giving blacks preference in hiring and promotion, or don't you have an opinion on this?" The other half of respondents heard the same question, except that the

Table 6.1. Perceptions of Black Assertiveness Have an Independent Effect on White Affirmative Action Attitudes

Affirmative action in employment

		b	SE (b)
	Warmth toward blacks	−.077	(.041)*
	Negative black stereotypes	−.043	(.049)
	Racial resentment	.389	(.033)***
	Assertive blacks	.055	(.024)**
	Constant	.633	(.046)***
	N = 1,531		
	R² = .129		

Quotas in education

		b	SE (b)
	Warmth toward blacks	−.149	(.046)***
	Negative black stereotypes	.055	(.055)
	Racial resentment	.577	(.038)***
	Assertive blacks	.089	(.027)***
	Constant	.375	(.052)***
	N = 1,494		
	R² = .226		

$* p < .10$ $** p < .05$ $*** p < .01$, two-tailed tests

Source: American National Election Study, 1992. All variables scaled 01. Analysis is OLS regression equation limited to white respondents.

Question wording:

Dependent measures

Affirmative action: Some people say that because of past discrimination, blacks should be given preference in hiring and promotion. Others say that such preference in hiring and promotion of blacks is wrong because it gives blacks advantages they haven't earned. What about your opinion—are you for or against preferential hiring and promotion of blacks? Do you [favor/oppose] preference in hiring and promotion strongly or not strongly?

Quotas: Some people say that because of past discrimination it is sometimes necessary for colleges and universities to reserve openings for black students. Others opposed quotas because they say quotas give blacks advantages they haven't earned. What about your opinion—are you for or against quotas to admit black students? Do you [favor/oppose] quotas strongly or not strongly?

Independent variables

Warmth toward blacks: I'd like to get your feelings toward some of our political leaders and other people who are in the news these days. I'll read the name of a person and I'd like you to rate that person using something we call the feeling thermometer. Ratings between 50 counterargument was attributed to "representatives of the black community" ("Others, such as representatives of the black community, say that because of past discrimination . . ."). This evocation of black assertiveness is intended to heighten group competition among whites. Moreover, in New Jersey, this reference is realistic given the very public advocacy work of black leaders and organizations on the racial profiling issue.

The hypothesis here is that highlighting black assertiveness will evoke white opposition more effectively where the assertiveness appears to violate the principle of race neutrality (affirmative action) than where it is a request for race neutrality (racial profiling). In other words, on an issue where race-neutral logic leads to policies favorable to blacks, the effect of racial competition over resources should be more subdued, if evident at all. On policies where the race-neutral logic works against efforts to help blacks, however, the ability to induce racial competition should be much greater.

This expectation is borne out, as seen in Table 6.2. Just hearing of affirmative action advocated by black leaders contributes to greater white opposition to the policy; a sizable, statistically significant difference emerges

---

degrees and 100 degrees mean that you feel favorable and warm toward that person. Ratings between 0 degrees and 50 degrees mean that you don't feel favorable toward the person and that you don't care too much for that person. You would rate the person at the 50 degree mark if you don't feel particularly warm or cold toward the person. If we come to a person whose name you don't recognize, you don't need to rate that person. Just tell me and we'll move on to the next one. How about blacks?

Negative stereotypes about blacks (two questions): Now I have some questions about different groups in our society. I'm going to show you a 7-point scale on which the characteristics of the people in a group can be rated. In the first statement a score of 1 means that you think almost all of the people in that group tend to be "hard-working." A score of 7 means that almost all of the people in the group are "lazy." A score of 4 means that you think that most people in the group are not closer to one end or the other, and of course you may choose any number in between. [Repeated for intelligent/unintelligent and peaceful/violent. Coded such that negative traits take on high values.]

Racial resentment (four questions): 1) Generations of slavery and discrimination have created conditions that make it difficult for blacks to work their way out of the lower class. 2) It's really a matter of some people not trying hard enough; if blacks would only try harder they could be just as well off as whites. 3) Irish, Italian, Jewish and many other minorities overcame prejudice and worked their way up. Blacks should do the same without any special favors. 4) Over the past few years blacks have gotten less than they deserve. [5-point agree/disagree responses. Questions 2 and 3 reverse coded.]

Assertive civil rights leaders: Some people say that the civil rights people have been trying to push too fast. Others feel they haven't pushed fast enough. How about you? Do you think that civil rights leaders are trying to push too fast, are going too slowly, or are they moving at about the right speed?

Table 6.2. The Black Opinion Leader Experiment

	Counterargument offered by generic others	Counterargument offered by "representatives of the black community"
Affirmative action		
Against policy	41%[a]	52%[a]
For policy	17	13
Don't know	42	36
	(311)	(281)
Racial profiling		
Good policy	27%[b]	30%[b]
Bad policy	49	46
Don't know	24	25
	(292)	(292)

[a] The increase is significant ($p < .05$).

[b] The increase is not significant ($p < .44$).

Note: Numbers in parentheses indicate number of respondents.

Source: The *Newark Star-Ledger*/Eagleton-Rutgers Poll. Sample is New Jersey adults eighteen and over. The first survey (affirmative action) was in the field November 1999. The second survey (racial profiling) was in the field February–March 2000. Statistical tests exclude "don't know" responses.

Question wording:

I'd like to ask you a question on the issue of giving minorities preferences in job hirings and promotions. Some say that such preferences are wrong because they give blacks advantages they haven't earned. Others (such as representatives of the black community) say that because of past discrimination, blacks should be given such preferences. How about you? Are you for or against giving blacks preference in hiring and promotion, or don't you have an opinion on this?

There has been some talk here in New Jersey about the practices of profiling—where police target certain cars to stop based on the race or age of people in the cars. Some say profiling makes sense because it increases our safety by stopping those people who are more likely to commit crimes. Others (such as representatives of the black community) object to the policy because they believe it unfairly discriminates against minorities who are pulled over because of their race or ethnicity. How about you? Do you think profiling is a good or bad policy for the State Police to use, or don't you have an opinion on this?

between the two experimental treatments. The difference is expected, for the presence of black advocates in the question is a subtle but real reminder that group interests clash. For the racial profiling question, the difference is slight, less than one-third the magnitude, and is quite possibly due to chance variation. This suggests that it is much more difficult to experimentally evoke group conflict on this issue, where the logic of race neutrality favors black and minority interests. Given the influence of race neutrality on these two issues, it is not surprising that white support for affirmative action is considerably lower than white opposition to racial profiling practices.

The divergent pattern has some theoretical implications. Scholars have begun to resolve inconsistent findings with respect to group conflict (e.g., Glaser 1994 and Giles and Hertz 1994, as compared to Oliver and Mendelberg 2000) by identifying conditions under which realistic group conflict does and does not affect racial attitudes. For instance, it seems the clash of interests has a larger impact on those individuals whose group faces the threat of loss more than those belonging to groups looking at gain (cf. Kahneman and Tversky 1984). Furthermore, people must recognize the clash of interests. Misperception of the racial environment or misunderstanding of a policy or a circumstance could mean that individual attitudes are not influenced by a group conflict context or situation.

The results above hint at an additional factor that could help predict where group conflict dynamics are most likely to flourish: whether or not the option favorable to blacks calls for racial groups to be treated differently. In such cases, group conflict responses coincide with a desire to protect the standard of equal treatment. Where equal treatment and group protection are at odds, on the other hand, a group conflict orientation has more difficulty getting established and equal treatment is quite likely to win out. In the Black Opinion Leader Experiment, we show that the effect emerges in the context of a race-conscious policy like affirmative action. In the context of racial profiling, however, where group interests may in fact be at stake but where the decision rule is to treat people of all groups the same, group conflict impulses are much more subdued.

The 4 Percent Solution

Thus far, we have looked at race-neutral logic as something that can mitigate the emergence of a group conflict orientation. But can the principle of race neutrality actually change people's minds? In 1999, the University of California attempted to make admissions preferences more palatable to the general public by recasting them in a race-neutral way; this was the inspiration for our next set of experiments.

The 1996 passage of Proposition 209 (the California Civil Rights Initiative), which banned state institutions from practicing affirmative action, led many to predict that the University of California system would lose significant racial and ethnic diversity. The state university system was and is considered by many to be the premier state-sponsored university system in the country.[3] If the most prestigious university system located in the most diverse state in the country lost much of its student diversity, this would be a major blow to efforts to increase minority representation at top institutions of higher education.[4]

The 1997 admissions season showed that these concerns were well founded. No longer able to use affirmative action to assess students, the drop was particularly pronounced at the flagship Berkeley campus; far fewer African American and Hispanic students were admitted than the year before, their spots absorbed by whites and Asian Americans. The 66 percent drop in the number of black admissions and the over 50 percent drop in Hispanic admissions led university officials to consider some new strategies to accomplish diversity. Some lawsuits were pending, but these challenges were very uncertain and would take a long time to be resolved.

The election of a new governor, Democrat Gray Davis, in 1998 gave those seeking to address this problem a powerful new advocate. Indeed, in his inaugural address in January 1999, Davis identified diversity at the state universities as a major concern. He announced that he would support a proposal, under discussion since the ill-fated 1997 admissions season, to assure acceptance to all students who finished in the top 4 percent of their class in California public high schools. Starting by linking this proposal to shared values, he then announced his support for the 4 percent solution:

> Californians are a fair and compassionate people. They believe in equality and justice. They are also a people of great decency and integrity. Our mission is to apply these principles to enhance opportunity for every Californian from every background and nationality. Under my administration, for example, we will seek to ensure diversity and fair play by guaranteeing to those students who truly excel by graduating in the top four percent of their high school—whether it's in West Los Angeles or East Palo Alto—those kids who excel will automatically be admitted to the University of California. (Davis 1999)

The idea that Davis embraced had many features that increased the breadth of its appeal. Racially neutral on its face, it still promised that high-achieving black and Hispanic students with lower test scores and fewer Advanced Placement opportunities would have a better chance of admission. Because it extended to similarly situated white and Asian students, the policy could not even be characterized as having a purely race-focused effect. The 4 percent solution also created a stronger incentive for students at poorly resourced state high schools to reach for University of California acceptance. No longer were these students competing with students from schools across the state. Finally, a similar policy had just come into practice in Texas following a court case that banned affirmative action in state university enrollments. The Texas policy seemed to be publicly accepted and relatively effective at promoting diversity in the first admission cycles. If it could win support in Texas, it certainly had a chance in California.

The 4 percent solution also had some serious drawbacks. For the policy to contribute to racial and ethnic diversity, it assumed racially segregated schools with predominantly black or Hispanic high schools contributing the successful black and Hispanic applicants. In reality, of course, schools are often very homogeneous, but segregated high schools are not a desirable foundation upon which to build future admissions policy. Also, recent analyses pointed to some possibly disquieting results of the Texas plan, specifically that white students strategically decided to attend public school rather than more competitive magnet schools, with an eye toward more easily reaching the 10 percent threshold operating in that state. The result, according to one analysis, was a net decrease in minority students' representation in the top 10 percent pool (Cullen, Long, and Reback 2011). The 4 percent solution also did nothing for admissions to law, medical, or other graduate programs. The concept simply could not be replicated at that level, yet a diverse corps of doctors, lawyers, academics, and other professionals is indeed a priority of those advocating affirmative action in education. Perhaps the biggest challenge to the 4 percent solution is that the university would now be admitting students from poor schools who were less prepared for a rigorous college curriculum than minority students coming out of stronger high schools. Without advanced courses and the kind of preparation received at better-resourced schools, many minority students were at a disadvantage upon arriving at Berkeley or one of the other University of California campuses. Without programming in place to help them catch up, these students were at an academic disadvantage next to students prepared at better schools.

Those problems aside, the 4 percent solution was advocated by many in California who saw it as a practical and politically palatable way to reverse the decline in diversity that the University of California system was already experiencing. Not only did Governor Davis rhetorically embrace the concept, but he used the prestige of his office to push change, lobbying the University of California regents at every opportunity. "If you've got the guts, the heart, the will and the determination to be in the top 4 percent, you're going to be a very good student at the University of California, and we will now have the mechanism to attract these students," said a jubilant Davis after the regents approved the policy (Burdman 1999). Davis so liked the ability to promote diversity in a race-neutral way that harnessed individualism and just deserts that the principle of neutrality informed some of his other policy decisions. He even vetoed a bill to create a program to encourage women and minorities to apply for state jobs. Such a program would violate Proposition 209, said Davis, and he preferred outreach programs "based on socioeconomic status, geographic area or other areas not based on race (akin to the merit-based admissions program at the University of California)" (Jordan 1999).

The 4 percent solution did appear to change the enrollment patterns of the University of California. Black and Hispanic enrollment rose to pre–Proposition 209 levels, although students were distributed across the U.C. campuses differently. Because the flagship schools had somewhat higher standards than the other U.C. schools, the 4 percent solution created more diversity in the second-tier U.C. schools like Irvine, Riverside, and Santa Cruz, but left Berkeley and UCLA with fewer blacks and Hispanics. From the perspective of those who most value diversity in the universities, the 4 percent solution has thus not been a panacea, but it has improved the situation and for that, even its critics have acknowledged its value.

Race Neutrality and Affirmative Action

To investigate whether the principle of race neutrality can win over whites, we utilize a two-stage persuasion experiment in the style of such scholars as Paul Sniderman and Thomas Piazza (1993), James Gibson (1998), and Katherine Tate (2003), and quite similar to the experiment we present in Chapter 3. As in the South Carolina study, the approach here is to gauge respondents' opinions with an initial question and then examine what sorts of counterarguments "ply them off" that position. This approach allows us to test the effect of bringing different considerations to the front of people's minds (Zaller and Feldman 1992) and to compare the impact on respondents' positions of raising different considerations. Many issue positions expressed on surveys, of course, are not hard and fast but change if concerns are allayed and/or questions are raised.

The persuasion experiment we conducted in California starts out by asking all the Field Poll respondents their position on the "use of quotas to improve educational opportunities for Blacks and Hispanics in California." It raises the point that "the percentage of Blacks and Hispanics in the University of California system is far lower than the percentage of Blacks and Hispanics in the state's overall population" before asking whether respondents "favor or oppose establishing quotas to guarantee Blacks and Hispanics better representation in the University of California system." The question thus balances the disproportionate racial balance in the university system with the visceral response the word "quota" often elicits. While one-third of white, non-Hispanic respondents favor establishing quotas "to guarantee Blacks and Hispanics better representation in the University of California system," 57 percent reject them. Almost 10 percent of respondents opt out of the question altogether. This distribution of responses is roughly similar to the distribution of responses on related public opinion questions posed to national samples (Steeh and Krysan 1996, 149). Racial preferences in the form of educational quotas are rejected by a large majority of white respondents.

The persuasion experiment moves forward only with those who reject the quotas in this first question. Half of these people, a randomly selected half, are probed further with an alternative race neutral, class-based plan (like the 4 percent solution) to bring the proportion of minorities in the university system more in line with the general population: "Suppose that there was a plan to increase the percentage of black and Hispanic students in the University of California system by giving students from poorer backgrounds more consideration. That way more blacks and Hispanics could be admitted without relying upon racial quotas. Would you then favor or oppose this plan to improve black and Hispanic representation in the University of California system?"Offered this alternative, many respondents do change course. More than one-third of quota opponents (36 percent) agree to this plan even though its explicit goal is to improve black and Hispanic representation (see Table 6.3). While just over half (53 percent) of the original opponents remain opposed, combining initial proponents with the new proponents now forms a majority. The race-neutral conceptualization does contribute to whites softening their views. It is persuasive. And the raw

Table 6.3. The Expanding-Pie Experiment

Favor or oppose quotas to guarantee blacks and
Hispanics better representation in state university

Favor quotas (%)	33
Oppose quotas (%)	57
Don't know (%)	9
	(593)

Attempts to persuade the 57% who oppose quotas

	Race-conscious, expanding pie	Race-neutral, fixed pie
Favor new plan (%)	24	36
Oppose new plan (%)	72	53
Don't know (%)	5	11
	(170)	(170)

Source: The Field Institute. Sample is a random sample of 1,003 California adults. The survey, conducted by telephone in either English or Spanish, was in the field June 9–18, 2000. This analysis is restricted to white, non-Hispanic respondents.

Question wording:
On another topic is the use of quotas to improve educational opportunities for blacks and Hispanics in California. Currently, the percentage of blacks and Hispanics in the University of California system is far lower than the percentage of blacks and Hispanics in the state's overall population. Do you favor or oppose establishing quotas to guarantee blacks and Hispanics better representation in the University of California system?

Race-conscious expanding pie (asked of half of quota opponents): Suppose that there was a plan to increase the total number of students in the University of California system and to reserve these additional spots for black and Hispanic students. That way more blacks and Hispanics could be admitted without taking the place of whites and Asians. Would you then favor or oppose establishing quotas to assure blacks and Hispanics greater representation in the University of California system?

Race-neutral fixed pie (asked of half of quota opponents): Suppose that there was a plan to increase the percentage of black and Hispanic students in the University of California system by giving students from poorer backgrounds more consideration. That way more blacks and Hispanics could be admitted without relying upon racial quotas. Would you then favor or oppose this plan to improve black and Hispanic representation in the University of California system?

material exists to change the outcome on the question of black and Hispanic representation in universities.

Race neutrality means that decisions about the allocation of resources should be made without consideration to race. Do whites believe in race neutrality because they believe that decisions should be made this way? Or do they believe in race neutrality because they think that whites will win larger shares of resources, whether those resources are seats in a university, contracts from the government, or jobs from the public or private sector?

The second half of the persuasion experiment offers a way to gauge whether support for race neutrality stems from principle or instead comes from a belief that whites benefit under race-neutral designs. We utilize a second set of arguments intended to talk respondents out of their antiquota position. Where, in the first follow-up, the plan is race neutral in design but favorable to minorities in outcome, in our second follow-up, we describe a plan that turns this formula on its head. Here, in what we call the expanding-pie plan, affirmative action opponents are offered a race-conscious solution (indeed a set of quotas), but one that does not require whites to give up spots to accommodate blacks. Specifically, respondents are asked whether they would support a plan that would increase the number of overall seats in the university and guarantee the additional seats for blacks and Hispanics. To do so would make it possible to improve proportionality in a race-conscious way but without any absolute loss to whites.

The expectation here is that we should see a difference in the persuasiveness of the race-conscious plan, which does not require white loss, and the race-neutral plan, which does require white loss.[5] If support for neutrality is simply based on assessments of losses, the race-conscious expanding-pie argument should yield the same amount of persuasion as the race-neutral argument, or perhaps even more. On the other hand, if support for the principle of race neutrality is genuine, more persuasion should take place when respondents are offered the race-neutral plan than the race-conscious one.

As Table 6.3 shows, the race-neutral framing is more effective at swaying respondents from their original skepticism, with 36 percent of original respondents favoring the race-neutral alternative but only 24 percent favoring the race-conscious alternative. Far fewer oppose the race-neutral plan outright (53 percent versus 72 percent). The difference between the two treatments, as shown in Table 6.4, achieves statistical significance ($p < .01$). Those who opt out of the question ("don't know") are removed from this analysis, modestly enhancing the difference between the two treatments. This difference, which we will call a persuasion gap, measures the difference in the power of the two arguments, and the race-neutral argument wins out even when there is a cost to whites associated with it.

It is noteworthy that about one-quarter of the whites who reject quotas in the first question accept them when offered the expanding-pie alternative.

Table 6.4. Subgroup Responses to the Expanding-Pie Experiment

	Proportion Supporting Preferences	
	Race-conscious, expanding pie	Race-neutral, fixed pie
All whites	.24	.40
	(165)	(157)
t	—	3.11***
People with children	.17	.40
	(45)	(45)
t	—	2.47**
People without children	.27	.40
	(119)	(111)
t	—	2.09**
Less educated	.23	.38
	(86)	(82)
t	—	2.03**
College degree +	.25	.41
	(86)	(82)
t	—	2.22**
Conservatives	.16	.23
	(63)	(49)
t	—	.91
Moderates / liberals / no ideology	.30	.48
	(102)	(108)
t	—	2.71***
	$* p < .10$ $** p < .05$	$*** p < .01$

Source: The Field Institute. Sample is a random sample of 1,003 California adults. The survey, conducted by telephone in either English or Spanish, was in the field June 9–18, 2000. This analysis is confined to white, non-Hispanic respondents. Cells represent the likelihood of accepting the compromise in response to one of the two follow-up arguments (respondents without an opinion are eliminated from the analysis).

The objection for these individuals is thus not quotas per se, for they explicitly agree to them in the follow-up question, but the sacrifice required of whites to accomplish racial proportionality. Where that sacrifice disappears, some whites relent, as one might expect from a group conflict orientation. The logic of this position is not malicious, but neither does it appear to stem from a principled commitment to race neutrality.

One can conclude from these results that the principle of race neutrality is genuinely held. We can examine other evidence that might substantiate this conclusion. If race neutrality is really embraced in a principled way, this gap should exist for both people with a perceived stake in university admissions and those without such a stake. That is, it should not be the case that some people—those without much personal interest in university admissions—can afford to be principled, while others cannot.[6]

Do people respond to the principle in a similar way even if they have a competitive stake in maintaining privilege? To answer this question, we look at how respondents in different subgroups respond to our two experiments: less-educated versus better-educated respondents, and respondents who have children under eighteen versus those without school-aged children. It is not difficult to imagine that better-educated people, defined here as those having a college degree, are more likely to perceive that they have a personal stake in university admissions than less educated people. Not only have they attended college themselves, but they are much more likely than less educated people to send their children to college.[7] They also tend to see more value in higher education. In a survey of southerners, for instance, 62 percent of college graduates and 42 percent of high school graduates agree with the proposition that "a college education is worth what it costs in time and money to [people] who are not going into professions" (Southern Focus Poll 1998). This is not to say that the less educated do not have any stake in university admissions, but rather that large numbers of well-educated whites, a broad swath of middle- and upper-middle-class people, are liable to connect higher education to their own self-interest and group interests. Along these same lines, people with school-aged children should be much more likely than those without children to perceive the issue from a more personal perspective, as anyone working in or around a university can attest.

What does the persuasion gap between the two counterarguments look like for these four different (overlapping) groups of respondents? Again, if the gap is really driven by principle, the experiment should work irrespective of whether it is conducted among those with a greater perceived interest in admissions or those without that perceived interest. This is the case (see Table 6.4). The gap between responses to the race-neutral counterargument and the race conscious counterargument is the same for less educated and better-educated respondents. It is, in fact, a bit smaller for those without children (without a stake) than for those with children. And the gap is statistically significant among all four subgroups. This further supports the notion that whites genuinely hold to the principle of race neutrality.

Remarkably, one subgroup that appears not to respond to the experiment in the same way is self-identified conservatives. Given the prominence of individualism and race neutrality in conservative rhetoric, one might expect the race-neutral framing to be particularly resonant among conservatives. It appears to be quite the opposite. Just where the persuasion gap might have been largest, it is smallest, with conservatives exhibiting only a seven-percentage-point difference compared to eighteen percentage points among other respondents. Given that conservative leaders generally have used race-neutral arguments against affirmative action and even have attempted to transform the argument into an alternative policy, it is striking that conservative respondents do not find the race-neutral plan much more convincing than the race-conscious plan to help blacks and minorities. The modest number of conservatives in our sample precludes putting too much stock in the result, but there is reason to suppose that the messages of conservative leaders on this issue are best received not by their base but by those less aligned with them.

The general argument flowing through this project is that if we account for how political competition and even threat affect how people think about racial-political issues, if we can mitigate the effects of competition and threat, perhaps we can design solutions that can win broader support for measures that benefit blacks and other disadvantaged minorities. The fact that the race-conscious/expanding-pie argument wins some converts (one-fourth of those who encounter it) suggests that people will respond to efforts to diminish the effects of group competition even if race-conscious methods are still employed. That the race-neutral/fixed-pie argument pulls even more people away from their first position does not diminish the fact that the expanding-pie argument is quite persuasive. It could be even more persuasive, we suspect, if "preferences" replaced "quotas" in the question. Nonetheless, the important point here is that political solutions that diminish racial competition can change people's minds.

The Art of the Possible

The sociologist William Julius Wilson (1990, 1999) has long advocated identifying race-neutral ways to advance minority interests, not just because of

majority white resistance to race-conscious policies but because such policies do not always reach those minorities who need help most. The results
from this chapter generally support Wilson's intuition and indeed put some
meat on the bones of his observation. Americans—whites and minorities as
well—not only seem to believe in race-neutral policies but genuinely hold
this principle and apply it in a relatively consistent way. Moreover, a race-
neutral logic that works in favor of blacks and other minorities tends to
diminish the effects of group conflict. Strikingly, although race neutrality is
very much a part of conservative political rhetoric on issues like affirmative
action, conservatives appear least responsive to race-neutral alternatives.

Otto von Bismarck reputedly called politics "the art of the possible."
Changing racial policies requires constructing biracial coalitions. Those
interested in change might be well served to consider how people respond
to race neutrality as a principle in designing and marketing policies that
address political and economic inequalities.

CHAPTER 7

Changing Minds, If Not Hearts

> Unless opinions favourable to democracy and to
> aristocracy, to property and to equality, to co-operation
> and to competition, to luxury and to abstinence, to
> sociality and individuality, to liberty and discipline, and
> all other standing antagonisms of practical life, are
> enforced and defended with equal talent and energy,
> there is no chance of both elements obtaining their due.
> —John Stuart Mill, "On Liberty"

John Stuart Mill's essay "On Liberty" calls attention to one of the central mandates of political psychology, understanding the uneven ways that the opinions upon which democratic government relies develop and find expression. We began this book with the concern that, on matters of race, patterns of rhetoric and framing evoke group conflict thinking and, by extension, opposition to policies designed to help blacks and other minorities. They do so not occasionally or sporadically but systematically, putting minorities at a consistent disadvantage. However, we entertained a note of optimism: if patterns of thinking highlight a problem, they may also contain the seeds of a solution. Perhaps creative use of the tools of politics can bring new talent and energy to bear.

We hope that we have now presented ample evidence that it can. We conclude in this chapter with some reflections and implications. We begin with a methodological point concerning experiments in the social sciences. From there, we turn to substantive lessons extending from our results.

Iterative Experimentation

In a classic essay, John R. Platt (1964) advocated an approach to scientific investigation that he termed "strong inference." Drawing from Francis Bacon's writings on the scientific method, Platt argued that the factor that discriminated the disciplines that progressed quickly from the ones that progressed slowly was the extent to which they had systematized a repetitive back and forth between induction and deduction. The stagnant, plodding disciplines were method-oriented and inclined to feel their way haphazardly toward generalizations. The successful disciplines took a more problem-oriented approach. They identified gaps in understanding, plausible hypotheses to bridge them, and the critical tests that would discriminate among the competing explanations. In this way, progress becomes more regular, more algorithmic: "The difference between the average scientist's informal methods and the methods of the strong-inference users," Platt wrote, "is somewhat like the difference between a gasoline engine that fires occasionally and one that fires in steady sequence. If our motorboat engines were as erratic as our deliberate intellectual efforts, most of us would not get home for supper" (1964, 348).

In one illustrative metaphor, Platt likens scientific progress to climbing a tree. The climb is not unidirectional. Rather, each advance leads to a new fork of several branches, with experimental outcomes necessary to determine which of the potential paths is the true one. Platt called this model the "conditional inductive tree" (347) because it is possible to advance to a new fork only by excluding as implausible alternative hypotheses generated after the previous advance. The insight is that a person would not—could not—foresee all the relevant questions and tests at the beginning of an investigation. Each set of results answers some questions but raises many more.

Recently, Daniel Kahneman has advocated an appealing model of "adversarial collaboration" that incorporates thinking along these lines. Rather than "lob rhetorical grenades at one another" (Gilovich, Medvec, and Kahneman 1998, 602), under adversarial collaboration, scholars from opposing camps decide on a test that, ex ante, might discriminate between their perspectives. Part of the model acknowledges the hindsight that can come only after carrying out a first test. In one exercise in adversarial collaboration, Barbara Mellers, Ralph Hertwig, and Kahneman advise, "Accept in advance that the initial study will be inconclusive. Allow each side to propose an additional experiment to exploit the fount of hindsight wisdom that commonly becomes available when disliked results are obtained" (2001, Table 1).

Iterative thinking is clearly evident in the so-called hard sciences. Individual labs typically carve out niches, acquiring the funding, equipment, and expertise to investigate a specific area (electron transfer dynamics in photosynthetic reaction centers, to point to a real example). Perhaps because of disciplinary organization, or perhaps because of methodological constraints, the model seems less evident in the social sciences. Consider the case of political psychology. The discipline traces many of its modern foundations to interview and survey work conducted at midcentury by scholars at Columbia and the University of Michigan (e.g., Berelson, Lazarsfeld, and McPhee 1954; Campbell et al. 1960). The methods these scholars advanced collected new kinds of data and painted a picture of public opinion that had not been seen before, but their approaches were laborious, requiring weeks of systematic observation or omnibus national surveys. The norm became for the discipline to draw much of its evidence from benchmark efforts designed not to investigate a narrow question but to serve the discipline as a whole. (For instance, the American National Election Study, an omnibus survey that has provided data for thousands of research articles, has been fielded every two or four years.)[1] Omnibus surveys provide insights that no other method can, but they carry limitations: narrow, discriminating tests are less likely and, when they occur, the learning process unfolds much more slowly.

Omnibus efforts, however, are now one part of a much more diverse tool kit that invites focus on problems rather than methods. One trend of particular relevance has been for the discipline increasingly to draw its evidence from randomized experiments (Druckman et al. 2011), which are highly conducive to a strong inference approach. Where omnibus surveys (because of their expense) are often designed to test a slate of ideas, experiments can be more narrowly tailored to provide a sharp answer to a discrete theoretical question. They are often low in cost, making them feasible for a small team of researchers or even a solo scholar. In many cases they can be conducted rapidly, allowing for a more iterative exchange between the creative conjectural work that Platt calls "intellectual invention" and the execution of a critical test. Approached in this iterative way, experimentation is not only cheaper per individual study but also more economical in the sense that construction of the third test builds on the results of the second, which in turn benefited from the results of the first, and so on.

Several technological advances are likely to make a strong inference approach to political psychology even more feasible and attractive. One that we employ throughout this book is the ability to incorporate experiments into the sort of public opinion surveys that private organizations like newspapers and marketers carry out frequently. As we have shown (for instance, in Oklahoma), these can sometimes be executed such that they capture the dynamics that underlie an important, but ephemeral, political event. A second advance is the development of techniques to conduct large surveys, even nationally representative ones, over the Internet, lowering collection costs substantially.[2] Third, and most recently, firms such as Amazon .com have developed online labor markets that allow small-scale experiments to be conducted over the Internet among opt-in samples with unprecedented speed and at incredibly low expense (Berinsky, Huber, and Lenz 2012; Ryan and Miller-Karl 2011).

Iterative experimentation proved pivotal to some of the key findings we describe in this book. In Mississippi, for instance, a second experiment allowed us to test whether the increase in support for the school bond stemmed from additional specificity about how the funds would be spent or from the perceived increase in control over their allocation. In New Jersey, iterative experiments uncovered a crucial disjuncture in how group conflict dynamics unfold when the principle of race neutrality favors blacks, as opposed to when its logic works against them. In Michigan, the more pronounced results that emerged from a second experiment on racial preferences in the context of other admission preferences showed that the possible existence of a double standard needed to be illustrated baldly to have an effect. In short, there is much that we would not have learned if we conducted all of our tests at once.

So what *have* we learned from our tests? The preceding chapters provide lessons about which frames worked in the context of specific issues. Here, we look across our studies and to other work in an effort to draw out broader lessons. We focus on three tools that seem effective in minimizing group conflict: control, social influence, and standards of fairness.

Control

In our view, the Mississippi experiment illustrates how perceptions of threat and control interact to structure conflicts between groups. Whites strongly opposed omnibus bonds for school improvements, especially in places where blacks would be the primary beneficiaries. However, when we simulated a different choice—one in which voters could choose several intermediate options between the extremes—general support rose substantially. Why? We point to evidence that voters are not responding only to the specific items on the ballot, although there is some evidence of this. Rather, it seems the ability to choose from among several middle options changed the psychological dynamics of the decision.

A large literature has developed showing that perceptions of threat from out-groups contribute to protective responses. Part of this pattern may stem from a feeling within the majority group that it is on the brink of losing control, a sense that to make a concession is to start down a slippery slope. Voters may think, "If this now, then what next?" and feel obliged to hold the line against what could be a long series of demands. We see the sense of control afforded by the checklist ballot as a possible way to neutralize this pattern of thinking. A choice about whether to fund programs becomes a choice about which programs most deserve funding. Voters get to decide for themselves which activities are worth the cost and register opposition to those that seem excessive.

Most political outcomes are not determined by referenda, so where else might control dynamics come into play? One possible place is in the structure of choices about candidates. Political science has an expansive literature analyzing how different ways to run elections influence who wins in politics. A particularly fruitful line of inquiry elucidates how different ways of structuring choices—single member vs. multimember districts, plurality vs. majority winners, cumulative voting, and so on—have real and important consequences for outcomes (Riker 1988). Much of this work suggests that minorities would do better under many of the alternatives to the rigid single-member, first-past-the-post elections that prevail in U.S. congressional elections. For instance, Elisabeth Gerber, Rebecca Morton, and Thomas Rietz (1998; see also Bowler, Donovan, and Brockington 2003) show that, if voters have two votes that they can either split between two candidates or lump onto a single preferred candidate, minority candidates are often more likely to win. Likewise, Douglas Amy (2002) argues that if the United States were to implement a proportional representation system (popular throughout Europe) it would increase representation of women and minorities.

Much of the past work analyzes election systems through the lens of rationality: it posits that each voter has stable preferences and full understanding of the election system. Voting decisions follow mechanically and deterministically from the pursuit of self-interest. Our perspective adds a psychological complement to the virtues the earlier work finds in alternative arrangements. Where the past work takes preferences as given, our results suggest that the choice structure can change preferences, making equivalent options seem more attractive under some circumstances. The pattern we identify, to be clear, seems to reinforce the prevailing wisdom: both proportional representation and cumulative voting are approaches likely to increase perceptions of control. Thus, in addition to channeling self-interest to more representative electoral outcomes, they may lower psychological resistance to alternatives that favor minorities.

The Mississippi results also provide a new, complementary perspective for past work on primary elections. The diffuse nature of election administration in the United States has allowed myriad methods of selecting party nominees to develop. There are closed primaries, where voters affiliate with a party and can vote only in their own party's nomination contest; blanket primaries, where voters can vote in the various nomination contests irrespective of their own party affiliation; and nonpartisan primaries, where candidates do not run in separate contests by party but rather one general contest, with the top two vote-getters proceeding to a runoff election.[3] Even within these schemes, there are differences in how much of an investment party affiliation represents—sometimes affiliating with a party can be done on Election Day, sometimes it must be done far in advance—and whether independents are allowed to participate.

Of course, each variation has implications for what sort of candidate is likely to lose or win. An important finding is that the nonpartisan systems, in which Republicans and Democrats run in the same primary contest, tend to elect more centrist candidates (Gerber and Morton 1998). There are several reasons why this tendency would emerge. For one, compared to the party-specific contests, candidates in nonpartisan contests need to appeal to a wider array of voters, which means extreme positions are likely to alienate important segments of the electorate and centrist positions are likely to be more attractive. The psychological dynamics that emerge in Mississippi illustrate a second factor that may be at work, one that comes not from the candidates but from the voters. Whereas in closed primaries, voters choose from candidates that lie along only part (about half) of the ideological spectrum, the voters in nonpartisan primaries enjoy a much wider set of choices, often ranging from extremely liberal to extremely conservative. The broader array may cast options in a different light. For a Republican voter, for instance, a staunch conservative may seem more extreme when viewed in the context of the fuller set of choices, whereas a moderate conservative may seem more appealing when evaluated against the specter of an ideologically distant liberal. For these reasons, open primaries may work through voter psychology to encourage moderate choices.

Much can be said in favor of moderation and compromise in politics. Moderate policy positions minimize the degree to which segments of citizens feel alienated. They increase policy stability, making it less likely for changes in leadership to precipitate drastic policy deviations. Political confrontation, especially when ostentatious, disenchants citizens with politics (Hibbing and Theiss-Morse 1995; Mutz and Reeves 2005). An affinity for moderation was woven into America's political fabric, with numerous political institutions intentionally designed to dampen rapid changes. We show an additional way that choice structure can encourage moderation. It can do so by channeling equivalent preferences to more moderate outcomes (as previous work shows), but also by changing how equivalent choices are perceived.

The finding is timely. There is mounting evidence that politicians are more divided and antagonistic than the voters they represent (Fiorina and Abrams 2008) and that elite polarization makes it difficult to address public policy concerns (McCarty, Poole, and Rosenthal 2008). Perhaps heresthetics can serve a palliative function by nurturing moderation and compromise. We think the election systems discussed above are one illustration, but there are other potential applications: Does the take-it-or-leave-it choice presented by most referenda obscure opportunities for compromise? Would our image of public opinion look somewhat different if pollsters presented voters with more finely grained choices? There is plenty of room for research and experimentation on these and other questions.

Social Influence

The second tool we highlight concerns how voters respond to the opinions of others around them. We are certainly not the first to investigate these effects. Consider, for instance, a folk wisdom that emphasizes the importance of momentum. It is routine for news coverage of elections not only to mention relative standing in polls but also who seems to be gaining or losing ground. The use of such gerunds implies a pattern: polling changes in one period predict similar changes in the next period; people respond to the opinions of others. Scholarship recognizes the pattern, too, in numerous studies on what has been termed the "bandwagon effect," a general tendency for voters to flock to the candidate who leads in the polls (Cook and Welch 1940;

Ansolabehere and Iyengar 1994; Mehrabian 1998; Blais, Gidengil, and Nevitte 2006). In other words, there appears to be a significant social basis to opinions about political candidates.

What is rather less clear is why the bandwagon effect occurs. Larry Bartels (1988, 108–112) provides a useful slate of four potential mechanisms to consider (see also Kenney and Rice 1994). First, it could occur for strategic reasons. Suppose an individual prefers candidate A to candidate B and, in turn, prefers candidate B to candidate C. If candidate B substantially leads candidate A in the polls, it might make sense to vote for candidate B—despite being the second choice—because a vote for A would be wasted, while a vote for B is potentially pivotal in the race between B and C. Second, individuals turn to other voters as a cue, a shortcut for deciding where their interests lie without having to evaluate policy positions. Third, voters could exhibit contagion, a tendency to get swept up, uncritically, in the excitement that comes when a candidate is mentioned more in the news and more enthusiastically by friends and neighbors. Fourth, voters might tend to support a winner—that is, they might seek "the gratification of a rational, apolitical spectator enjoying vicarious involvement in the horse race for its own sake," even if it means voting for someone "about whose substantive qualities they have no illusions" (Bartels 1988, 112). Patrick Kenney and Tom Rice (1994) find some evidence in favor of each of these mechanisms, while Diana Mutz (1997) layers additional complexity by proposing a fifth mechanism: when a candidate is ahead in the polls, voters who originally preferred someone else hear and absorb new reasons to support him or her, causing them to revise their original preferences.

These possibilities are not exclusive. There is probably at least a bit of truth to each of them. It is hard to understand how each mechanism works because, in general, they all occur simultaneously. Yet a nuanced understanding is important because social influence dynamics speak to broader questions about voter sophistication, candidate viability, and the use of campaign resources.

Our results from South Carolina contribute to the discussion. By focusing attention on an issue rather than a person, we can go far in isolating one of the proposed routes of social influence—cue taking. To see how, consider the evidence that people who were originally opposed to removing the Confederate flag from the state capitol become more supportive of removal when it is supported by a majority of voters. A strategic bandwagon effect does not seem to explain the pattern here, because we ask the respondents about their ideal preference, not which option they would vote for. That is, unlike a candidate election, it is not a situation in which supporting one's first choice could have the unwelcome effect of bringing about the least-preferred outcome. The learning mechanism described by Mutz does not seem to explain the result, either, since we do not provide respondents with new information about any proposal. Moreover, the possibility of support-ing a winner becomes less likely in the context of an issue (rather than a candidate) opinion, because an issue outcome would not seem to have the same emotional payoff as an election outcome. Finally, contagion does not seem to be at play here, because we have done nothing to generate the excitement—more news coverage and so forth—that is central to the con-tagion hypothesis.

Cue taking remains, but it is working in an interesting way. Most scholarship on cue taking suggests it works by providing information about a policy. For instance, Arthur Lupia's (1994) study of California auto insurance referenda suggests that learning about public endorsements taught voters about the nature of the different reform proposals. More re-cently, John Bullock (2011) finds that cues have the most impact when there is a dearth of information about what policy alternatives do. Something dif-ferent seems to be going on in our South Carolina study. The elite compro-mise cue provides information about a policy; it signals to voters that experts who share their interests found a compromise palatable. But the elite cue does not appear to influence opinion. The majority compromise cue, which does influence opinion, also provides information, but of a different sort. It signals that the line of political division is not blacks versus whites but rather compromisers versus stalwarts; in short, it provides information well attuned to neutralize group conflict proclivities.

The pattern of change on one current issue, gay marriage, shows some hints that social dynamics may be at play. Consider that, in the sixteen years from 1988 to 2004, support for gay marriage increased only nineteen per-centage points, from 11 percent to 30 percent, a rate just above one point per year (Brewer and Wilcox 2005). By 2011, support reached a majority in a number of polls—for instance, Gallup put the figure at 53 percent—suggesting that the rate of change from 2004 to 2011 had more than doubled (Newport 2011). The much-increased rate of change suggests that more is at work than mere generational replacement; minds are changing on this emotional is-sue. Does press coverage of this trend lend it energy? Does learning about an ever broader base of public support lessen resistance to this (rather different) group conflict issue? We think this is possible and certainly merits investigation. Other questions are worthy of attention: What kind of information is provided by different sorts of cues? When are social-influence cues most persuasive? What sorts of people are most persuaded by them? And how much social support is enough to change a mind?

Double-Edged Swords

Examining the structure of white racial attitudes, Paul Sniderman and Thomas Piazza wrote that Americans "are moved by a swirl of concerns and principles in responding to contemporary issues of race" (1993, 110). Among the concerns were political ideology, principles of equal treatment, appraisals of whether blacks undertook a good-faith effort to solve problems, and, for some, prejudice. They argued that these considerations compete, with different ones emerging as more prevalent depending on the issue and circumstances. The pliability that Sniderman and Piazza document is consistent with the over-time instability in policy opinions noted by others (e.g., Converse 1970) as well as the feelings of conflict and ambivalence that voters express when asked how they think about fairness considerations in politics (Hochschild 1986).

The third tool we highlight stems from this swirl of concerns that provided the starting point for many of our tests. Several of the issues we study—affirmative action and reparations, for example—inherently pit two or more defensible fairness standards against each other. For instance, preferential college admission policies could be called unfair under the principle that when a person is being evaluated, the evaluation should not be influenced by his or her race. On the other hand, ending such policies could be called unfair on the idea that they are necessary to level the playing field for socioeconomically disadvantaged groups. By the same token, reparations could be construed as unfair because they require current taxpayers to pay for violations they did not commit, or they could be seen as necessary for fairness to the extent one believes it is unfair for victims to go uncompensated.

Other efforts have shown that calling attention to different concerns, as we do, can change opinions, so it is not earth-shattering that what has worked in the past has worked again here. Rather, our contribution is problem focused. We show how effective such framing can be in moving whites to positions that are more sympathetic to minorities. Our frames work, we argue, because they tap into previously unapplied but genuinely held principles. In Michigan, we called attention to the fact that removing racial preferences in college admission would create a double standard where some groups—such as children of alumni and full-pay students— would continue to benefit but racial minorities would not. Doing so led to huge changes in opinion. In Oklahoma, we cast reparations not as a symbolic gesture of restorative justice, but as an application of legal standards of retributive justice and just deserts that almost everyone endorses. Again, the framing specifics appeared to weaken opposition to concessions. In South Carolina, whites supported a political compromise favorable to blacks where it seemed to generate majority support—not because it represented a healing societal moment but out of respect for political power. In New Jersey, commitment to the principle of race neutrality attenuated group conflict patterns in the domain of racial profiling by police.

Looking across these examples, we note an ironic thread that binds them together, which is that all four of the fairness considerations we highlight— just deserts, retributive justice, majority rule, race neutrality—are conservative, at least inasmuch as they align with a conservative worldview and, incidentally, operate to preserve white advantages. Witness, for example, the use of majority rule to justify the political losses that minorities inevitably experience in the New South, a place where whites are overwhelmingly affiliated with the dominant Republican Party (Black and Black 2003). An important part of our argument is that there are two edges to most of these swords. Just as these principles highlight what made status-quo policies appealing in the first place, so too can they be reimagined and reimplemented to work in favor of racial equality. And that is possible because, for nearly everybody, the commitment to them is, in a fundamental sense, real.

The lesson is not banal or insignificant. It is all too easy to adopt a Manichaean view of politics in which the veracity and virtue of one's own opinions go without question while political opponents are assumed to have self-serving, ill-informed, nefarious, or otherwise base motives.[4] This view is wrong far more often than it is right, and it is not a useful starting point if one's objective is to persuade. In contrast, there is an approach that we think is far more constructive, not to mention a much better reflection of reality. It is to think about what values people share in common, and how they might have arrived at different conclusions even given similar values. Of all the principles and concerns that swirl around our minds, why did some win out over others, and how might it be otherwise?[5]

Hearts and Minds Revisited

The logic of group conflict theory helps us understand an important reason minorities so often face an uphill battle in generating public support for redress, why they might find themselves on the losing end of democratic politics, not occasionally but systematically. Group conflict thinking is not the only reason. The personality-focused perspectives mentioned above point to other contributing factors, as does work that emphasizes the ideological arguments that elites use to frame racial issues (e.g., Sniderman and Carmines 1997), and perhaps other schools of thought as well. If each of these perspectives has at least some leverage—if each gets at a piece of the puzzle—a natural question follows: if we wanted to change the politics of race, if we wanted to make inroads on these most important issues, where should we direct our energy?

One place we might start is with hearts, the deep feelings of apprehension, mistrust, resentment, or even hatred that seem to guide at least some people's opinions on racial issues. Characterizing work in this vein, Stuart Oskamp endorses this approach, writing that "finding ways to *reduce* prejudice and discrimination is *the* central issue in attacking racism in our society" (2000, vii, emphasis in original). Certainly if it were possible to alter the sentiments that underlie the opinions, it might change the pattern of results that seem to emerge.

In the introduction, we suggested that it is difficult to change hearts. We pointed, for instance, to how whites' feelings toward blacks as a group have remained almost unmoved from 1964 to 2008. Other investigations speak to that difficulty. After one recent review of nearly one thousand academic studies of prejudice reduction, Elizabeth Paluck and Donald Green (2009) lament, "In terms of size, breadth, and vitality, the prejudice literature has few rivals. Thousands of researchers from an array of disciplines have addressed the meaning, measurement, and expression of prejudice. The result is a literature teeming with ideas about the *causes* of prejudice. In quantitative terms, the literature on prejudice *reduction* is vast, but a survey of this literature reveals a paucity of research that supports internally valid inferences and externally valid generalization" (347, emphasis ours). The authors offer a methodological proposal—more field studies that test how ideas developed in a lab transfer to a naturalistic context—but the larger point is that if there is a potent medicament capable of soothing racial animosity by deliberate intervention, it has yet to be demonstrated in a convincing way.

We note also that the modest prejudice-reduction interventions that do seem to work are quite intensive. Green and Janelle Wong's (2009) study of the contact hypothesis involved a three-week wilderness trip with racially mixed camping groups. Greg Duncan and colleagues (2003) also find support for the contact hypothesis, but the intervention was to assign college students a minority roommate. Notable though these results are, it is difficult to imagine the interventions themselves being extended to influence large segments of the population, especially given the tendency for people to gravitate toward communities and social groups that are homogeneous with respect to both race and political views (Mutz 2002; Bishop 2009; Anderson 2010).

Then again, when it comes to who wins in politics, perhaps we do not need to change hearts. "The art of politics," wrote William Riker (1988, 209), is "to find some alternative that beats the current winner." With remarkable lucidity, he showed that political majorities, by their very nature, exist in a precarious state. They are constantly vulnerable to splintering and restructuring that can convert the minority of today into the majority of tomorrow. The restructuring need not come from persuasion as traditionally conceived; indeed, deep persuasion is probably exceptional. Neither need it sway huge swaths of voters; marginal changes can be crucial. Rather, the creative, entrepreneurial, and experimental task is to identify alternatives that are *already* attractive in some way, cast them so that they appeal to a majority of voters, and inject them into the contest of ideas. In this way, minds can change.

Such has been the project of this book. Our tests do not claim to have changed underlying sentiments but only (though often pivotally) the way they come to bear in politics. For this reason, the solutions we offer are certain not to be fully satisfying. They are not fully satisfying to us and leave unfinished the important work of erasing pernicious animosities that continue to persevere. Still, there are two things that remain to be said in their favor. First, what our solutions lack in idealism, they perhaps make up for in pragmatism. They are things that can be employed, and now, to change who wins in politics. Second, if by changing minds we mend some of the wounds that linger from a calamitous past, then maybe, if slowly, hearts would change as well.

NOTES

Chapter 1. Burdens of Our Past

1. A more recent analysis finds confirmation that coverage of the Reverend Wright scandal increased whites' negative feelings toward Obama (McKenzie 2011).

2. Nine individuals said the government should treat blacks better and fifteen that whites should be treated better.

3. Blacks constitute just 1.1 percent of all the members of Congress to have served throughout history (Manning and Shogan 2011).

4. These figures sum to just forty-nine states. This is because Nebraska has a unicameral legislature, which we consider with the upper houses.

5. For a fuller synopsis of related work, see Druckman and Lupia (2000).

6. For a book-length work that juxtaposes public opinion with a more enlightened notion of "public judgment," see Yankelovich (1991).

7. For a canonical discussion of group conflict theory, see Blumer (1958).

8. For a fuller explication of why the previous literature looking at these relationships is problematic, and how experimental findings address these problems, see Glaser (2003).

9. For an alternative measure of implicit attitudes that is currently gaining popularity, see Payne et al. (2005).

10. Kinder and Drake (2009) call attention to this feature.

11. Data limitations preclude us from tracing the gay and lesbian trend back farther than 1984, which likely would reveal an even lower baseline for this group.

12. Gaines, Kuklinski, and Quirk (2006) provide a helpful history of survey experimentation that called our attention to some of the examples we highlight here.

Chapter 2. Ballot Architecture and the Building of Schools

A previous version of this chapter was published as James M. Glaser, "White Voters, Black Schools: Structuring Racial Choices with a Checklist Ballot," *American Journal of Political Science* 46 (2002): 35–46.

1. Occasionally, there are members who, because of principle or political advantage, do force the issue to a vote.

2. Jackson was not unusual. Many school districts across the state found this threshold difficult to meet after 1964. The passage rate for all education bond issues between 1955 and 1965 was 88 percent. Only 49 percent passed between 1975 and 1989 (Walker 1991).

3. The second bond issue was a bit less ambitious, with supporters scaling down their request from $42 million to $29.75 million. Scaling down is a frequent response to a bond issue failure, though it did not help here.

4. Of course, elections such as the one in Jackson rely as much on motivating people to turn out to vote as on changing people's minds. The questions posed in this experiment do not really get at how much people might be motivated to participate in the two conditions, an interesting question but one beyond the scope of this study.

5. We have classified "don't know" responses to the omnibus question and "don't know" responses to all three of the items on the checklist as missing data. Our interpretation of those who opt out is that they are akin to nonvoters. It is possible that these people may be trying to avoid expressing their true opposition to these items (Reeves 1997, 87; Berinsky 1999). While this might make a difference in the overall levels of support for the schools, it is again the difference in the two treatments that is important here. Besides, respondents in the omnibus treatment opt out of the question at about the same rate as those in the checklist treatment.

6. For readers unfamiliar with the concept of statistical significance, it refers to standard tests used to determine the likelihood that a given difference would arise by chance. The p values we report here and elsewhere can be interpreted as the probability that a particular difference between groups would arise if the groups were really the same. Thus, asterisks in Table 2.3 signify that, using a difference of means test, the increase from 56 percent support for the omnibus measure to 74 percent for one of the checklist items almost certainly would not have arisen by chance. Instead, it arose because our treatment had an effect. There are a number of excellent resources where readers of all levels of sophistication can learn about this and other tests. One of our favorite resources is the Khan Academy, a compendium of free online videos that cover educational topics such as statistics. See http://www.khanacademy.org/math/.

7. Data on the racial distributions of districts and public schools within districts come from the Mississippi Department of Education. Data from the 1990s are no longer available on the department website, but more recent data are available at http://orsap.mde.k12.ms.us/MAARS/index.jsp.

8. We have conducted a second set of experiments that we will discuss in the next section. The group conflict results repeat, even more vividly, in these experiments (see Table 2.5).

9. An example of how voters view school bureaucracies came in a 1998 initiative election in California. Proposition 223 proposed to limit administrative spending to 5 percent of school budgets, the rest going to classroom use. The proposition failed after

a vigorous campaign against it, but Californians clearly found resonance in the message that the initiative would "get rid of bureaucratic bloat" (Asimov 1998). At the beginning of the campaign, internal polling had only 12 percent of voters opposed to the basic idea (Johnson 1998).

10. At one point, we did consider putting price tags on each item but rejected this for two reasons. First, it was not practical. The survey was conducted throughout Mississippi and school districts in the state vary so much in terms of size that the costs associated with each of these items also would differ greatly. There was a potential ethical problem with this plan as well. Indicating what the bond issue would cost might suggest that a real election was taking place when in fact it was not.

11. This is not a perfect test of the hypothesis. There is, unfortunately, no way to bring back in the possibility of money going for administrative and bureaucratic purposes in this part of the experiment. Furthermore, while this question wording still breaks down the funding targets more specifically, it is much less likely to evoke new considerations. Unlike the specific checklist case, these alternatives are not likely to raise considerations of overheated children or computerless classrooms.

Chapter 3. Following Neighbors, If Not Leaders

A previous version of this chapter was published as James M. Glaser, "Public Support for Political Compromise on a Volatile Racial Issue: Insight from the Survey Experiment," *Political Psychology* 27 (2006): 423–439.

1. Almost all the other southern states have had their own Confederate flag issues, from Confederate flags hanging in legislative chambers to Confederate symbols being incorporated into the official state flag. Nonetheless, South Carolina was the only state to fly the flag from such an official, prominent, and visible place.

2. An alternative considered by a black legislator and a white Republican leader was to raise the African liberation flag atop the capitol dome instead of taking the Confederate flag down. That proposal never came to be.

3. It did so in the context of a hard-fought Republican presidential primary campaign between George W. Bush and John McCain in which neither candidate spoke out against the flag or in favor of the proposals to bring it down. Later, McCain expressed regret for this, saying it was the one point in the campaign on which he succumbed to taking a popular stand over a principled stand: "Only once, I believe, did I act in an unprincipled way. But once is enough, and I want to tell the people of South Carolina and all Americans that I sincerely regret breaking my promise to always tell you the truth" (*New York Times* 2000).

4. Both surveys were designed to tap responses to the candidates in the upcoming Republican primary and little else. The survey contexts in which the experiments were conducted were virtually the same, allowing for the direct comparison of experimental results across the surveys. Moreover, our experiments were placed at the

top of the instruments, assuring that other questions would not affect the experimental results.

5. These data come from the same Mason-Dixon survey. This question about perception of the flag was asked after the compromise experiment; it clearly did not influence responses to the experiment.

6. One confused respondent was a flag opponent in the first round, a flag proponent in the second. Clearly the answer to one of these questions is wrong and we have removed this respondent from the analysis. There are a couple of other respondents like this in the experiments discussed in the next section and they also are purged.

7. On the other side, 70 percent of flag opponents also believe that a majority of South Carolinians stand with them.

8. Because the first survey is of all likely voters, the second of all likely Republican voters, the comparison is not perfect. Still, extracting flag proponents from both surveys, as we have done, focuses the analysis on comparable groups.

9. We are disappointed from a normative perspective but not an analytical one. Failed hypotheses too often go unreported due to a bias that infiltrates the academic process at every step—writing, reviewing, editing—leading to an unfortunate and misleading skew toward positive results (Sterling, Rosenbaum, and Weinkam 1995).

10. Governor Hodges lost his next election, and some commentators attributed this to the flag issue, but Hodges's position was always tenuous as a Democratic governor in a heavily Republican state.

Chapter 4. Remorse, Retribution, and Restoration

1. Another analysis of *negotiate/negotiation*, not included in Figure 4.1, shows a pattern similar to *compromise*.

2. Oklahoma is not the only place such an effort took place. In Florida and North Carolina, there also were efforts at reparations to victims of race riots from the early twentieth century. In Florida, the state legislature issued an apology and about $150,000 in payments to each of the eleven living survivors of a massacre in the town of Rosewood; it was the first payment of its kind. In North Carolina an apology was issued by the state Democratic Party, but it was not accompanied by any payments to survivors.

3. For some empirical work that compares the power of symbolic and material concessions in bridging political divides and attenuating conflict, see Ginges et al. (2007).

4. According to the lynching records at Tuskegee Institute, rape and attempted rape (more accurately, the accusation of rape) was the precipitating event for 27 percent of all incidents of lynching between 1916 and 1927. Homicide, the leading cause, was identified as the precipitating event in one-third of all lynchings (Williams 1970).

5. Franklin, one of the foremost experts on America's racial history and an advisor to President Clinton's Commission on Race, grew up in and near Tulsa. Indeed, his father lost his home in the riots (*New York Times* 1999a).

6. In a finding going back to the analysis of the tax revolts of the late 1970s and early 1980s, white antagonism to taxes is linked to symbolic racism and the idea that taxes from whites are supporting government programs for blacks and other minorities (Sears and Citrin 1982, 167–170).

7. The usual social science definition of "southern" is membership in the former Confederacy. Of course, Oklahoma was not a state in the mid-nineteenth century.

Chapter 5. A Panoply of Preferences

1. The "compensation for discrimination" rationale has a liability. If this is the aim of preferential policies, then why should they work *against* some groups that have been subject to discrimination, such as Asians and women?

2. For information on all these initiatives, see Larson and Menendian (2008).

3. See Kinder and Mendelberg (1995) and Kuklinski et al. (1997) for sharp explications of these two arguments.

4. Elsewhere, Kane uses a metaphor to describe this dynamic: "Suppose that there were one parking space reserved for disabled drivers in front of a popular restaurant. Eliminating the reserved space would have only a minuscule effect on the parking options for nondisabled drivers. But the sight of the open space may frustrate many passing nondisabled motorists looking for someplace to park" (2003, 573).

5. The data for these surveys are available online at http://www.ippsr.msu.edu/soss/SOSSdata.htm.

6. This analysis holds constant the apparent impact of sex and citizenship status.

7. The male-female ratio has some bearing on the experience of students of both sexes in terms of social life. For the university, a heavily skewed ratio is also problematic from the perspective of Title IX. The resources of the university, particularly in athletics, should reflect the ratio of men to women in the student body and this can be a problem when the more expensive and participatory sports are played by men.

8. For a thoughtful journalistic exposition of these trends, see Rosin (2010).

9. Tufts has long aspired to need-blind admissions (and in two recent years has accomplished a need-blind process), but this has not been sustainable.

10. We thank the Tufts University Office of Admissions for providing the data for these analyses.

11. Sometimes these winners and losers are quite unexpected. Ironically, while conservatives may dislike admissions preferences, the desire for ideological diversity on a college campus leads some admissions offices in "liberal" liberal arts colleges to practice affirmative action for conservatives. The educational experience for all, so

goes this logic, is enhanced when students do not all think alike and encounter others with differing points of view.

12. These findings are only partly consistent with Wilson et al. (2008). In their study, like ours, asking first about affirmative action for blacks appears to suppress support for affirmative action for women. Wilson et al., however, find that reversing the order so that affirmative action for women is asked first does raise support for racial preferences.

13. To accommodate all versions of the questions, and to have enough respondents in each "treatment," these questions are asked over the course of two surveys conducted on the same population within several months of each other. The time difference is insignificant enough so that it could not bias the results.

14. If a respondent approved of preferences for blacks or Hispanics in this battery of questions, they are coded as approving of racial preferences.

Chapter 6. A Spotlight on Race Neutrality

1. The California Field Poll is commercial while the New Jersey poll is part of a nonprofit institution affiliated with Rutgers University. The California Field Poll was conducted by the Field Institute with a representative sample of 1,003 California adults living in households with telephones. Interviews in English and Spanish were conducted in June 2000. The *Newark Star Ledger*/Eagleton Polls, using samples of New Jersey adults, were in the field in November 1999 and February–March 2000.

2. The high-quality interactions conjecture stems from so-called contact theories. See Stein, Post, and Rinden (2000) for one effort to disentangle the posited benefit of group contact from the posited harmful effects of group competition.

3. It is hard to systematically evaluate the standing of the system as a whole. Yet even in 2011, the *U.S. News and World Report* rates UC Berkeley and UC Los Angeles as the top two public universities in the country. UC San Diego, UC Davis, and UC Santa Barbara are also in the top ten, with UC Irvine ranked thirteenth (*U.S. News and World Report* 2012).

4. By some measures, such as the Sullivan Index, California is the country's most diverse state (Bernick 2011). According to the Census Bureau's diversity index (U.S. Census Bureau 2000), which calculates the percentage of times two randomly selected people would differ by race/ethnicity, it is actually ranked second behind Hawaii.

5. It might be suggested that whites might still lose something in the expanding-pie solution. Larger class sizes, for instance, could accompany this plan, altering the quality of the education whites might receive in the university. Moreover, they may gain something in the fixed-pie solution, namely a more diverse student body enriching the educational experience. But these are not considerations likely to come to mind in the context of a survey question.

6. Glaser (2001) shows, for instance, that well-educated whites are considerably more likely than less-educated whites to approve preferences, except in the case of

preferences in higher education, where they are significantly less supportive. This puzzle, we argue, stems in part from well-educated whites perceiving group interests to be more at stake on university admissions than on the other preference issues.

7. According to General Social Survey data (1972–1996), 54 percent of fathers with at least a bachelor's degree have children with at least a bachelor's degree (52 percent of mothers). Only 15 percent of fathers (16 percent of mothers) with a high school degree or less have children with at least a bachelor's degree.

Chapter 7. Changing Minds, If Not Hearts

1. A bibliography of research that employs ANES data, compiled in December 2010, includes over 5,700 citations. See http://electionstudies.org/resources/papers /reference_library.htm.

2. For instance, Knowledge Networks maintains a nationally representative survey panel. Another firm, YouGov/Polimetrix, argues that weighting techniques can be used to construct a nationally representative sample using opt-in recruiting.

3. Under nonpartisan primaries, it is possible for two candidates of the same party to face each other in the general election. Also, if one candidate receives an outright majority (more than 50 percent) in the first round, he or she wins the election and no second round is necessary.

4. Jonathan Haidt's (2012) synthesis of motivated reasoning and moral psychology represents a new and particularly compelling overview of the psychological mechanisms that underpin these tendencies.

5. To emphasize situational factors, as we do, is in the spirit of one of the grand traditions in social psychology (Ross and Nisbett 1991).

REFERENCES

Allen, Michael O., and Don Singleton. 1998. "Protest Shuts N.J. Turnpike." *New York Daily News*, May 17.

Allport, Gordon W. 1954. *The Nature of Prejudice*. Garden City, N.Y.: Doubleday Anchor Books.

———. 1962. "Prejudice: Is It Societal or Personal?" *Journal of Social Issues* 18 (2): 120–134.

Alvarez, R. Michael, and John Brehm. 1997. "Are Americans Ambivalent Toward Racial Policies?" *American Journal of Political Science* 41: 345–374.

American National Election Study, 1984–1994: Pre- and Post-Election Survey Files [machine-readable data files]. 1984–1994. Conducted by the Center for Political Studies of the Institute for Social Research, the University of Michigan, and the National Election Studies. Principal investigators, Steven J. Rosenstone, Donald R. Kinder, Warren E. Miller, and the National Election Studies. Ann Arbor: Inter-University Consortium for Political and Social Research.

American National Election Study, 1992: Pre- and Post-Election Survey [computer file]. 1993. Conducted by the Center for Political Studies and Inter-University Consortium for Political and Social Research, University of Michigan. Ann Arbor, Mich.: Inter-University Consortium for Political and Social Research.

American Political Science Association Plenary Session. 2000. "The Clinton Presidency: A Retrospective." September 1.

Amy, Douglas J. 2002. *Real Choices / New Voices: How Proportional Representation Elections Could Revitalize American Democracy*. New York: Columbia University Press.

Anderson, Elizabeth. 2010. *The Imperative of Integration*. Princeton, N.J.: Princeton University Press.

Ansolabehere, Stephen, and Shanto Iyengar. 1994. "Of Horseshoes and Horse Races: Experimental Studies of the Impact of Poll Results on Electoral Behavior." *Political Communication* 11: 1–19.

Ansolabehere, Stephen, Nathaniel Persily, and Charles Stewart III. 2010. "Race, Region, and Vote Choice in the 2008 Election: Implications for the Future of the Voting Rights Act." *Harvard Law Review* 123 (6): 1385–1436.

Arcidiacono, Peter, Esteban M. Aucejo, and Ken Spenner. 2011. "What Happens After Enrollment? An Analysis of the Time Path of Racial Differences in GPA and Major Choice." http: //seaphe.org.

Arkes, Hal R., and Philip E. Tetlock. 2004. "Attributions of Implicit Prejudice, or 'Would Jesse Jackson "Fail" the Implicit Association Test?'" *Psychological Inquiry* 15 (4): 257–278.

Asimov, Nanette. 1998. "Problems in L.A. Schools Driving Education Initiatives." *San Francisco Chronicle*, May 24.

Associated Press. 2000a. "Poll Finds Support for Removing Flag." January 10.

———. 2000b. "New Poll Shows Majority Want Confederate Flag Removed." January 21.

———. 2000c. "Poll Shows South Carolinians Support Senate Plan to Remove Confederate Flag." May 1.

Baca, Kim. 2000. "Confederate Flag Year's Top Story." *Associated Press*, December 25.

Banaji, Mahzarin R. 2001. "Implicit Attitudes Can Be Measured." In *The Nature of Remembering: Essays in Honor of Robert G. Crowder*, J. S. Nairne, I. Neath, and A. Surprenant, eds., 117–151. Washington, D.C.: American Psychological Association.

Barrett, Jennifer. 2003. "Bush Loses Ground." *Newsweek*, February 14.

Barstow, David, and David Kocieniewski. 2000. "Records Show New Jersey Police Withheld Data on Race Profiling." *New York Times*, October 12.

Bartels, Larry M. 1988. *Presidential Primaries and the Dynamics of Public Choice*. Princeton, N.J.: Princeton University Press.

Bauman, John F., Roger Biles, and Kristin M. Szylvian, eds. 2000. *From Tenements to the Taylor Homes: In Search of an Urban Housing Policy in Twentieth-Century America*. University Park: Pennsylvania State University Press.

Berelson, Bernard R., Paul F. Lazarsfeld, and William N. McPhee. 1954. *Voting: A Study of Opinion Formation in a Presidential Campaign*. Chicago: University of Chicago Press.

Berinsky, Adam J. 1999. "The Two Faces of Public Opinion." *American Journal of Political Science* 43: 1209–1230.

Berinsky, Adam J., Gregory Huber, and Gabriel Lenz. 2012. "Evaluating Online Labor Markets for Experimental Research: Amazon.com's Mechanical Turk." *Political Analysis* 20 (3): 351–368.

Bernick, Ethan M. 2011. "Population Diversity and Policy Diversity: Explaining State Choices in Medicaid Managed Care." *Journal of Policy Practice* 10: 307–325.

Bertrand, Marianne, and Sendhil Mullainathan. 2004. "Are Emily and Greg More Employable Than Lakisha and Jamal? A Field Experiment on Labor Market Discrimination." *American Economic Review* 94 (4): 991–1013.

Billig, Michael, and Henri Tajfel. 1973. "Social Categorization and Similarity in Intergroup Behaviour." *European Journal of Social Psychology* 3 (1): 27–52.

Bishop, Bill. 2009. *The Big Sort: Why the Clustering of Like-Minded America Is Tearing Us Apart*. New York: Mariner Books.

Black, Earl, and Merle Black. 2003. *The Rise of Southern Republicans*. Cambridge, Mass.: Belknap Press.

Blais, Andre, Elisabeth Gidengil, and Neil Nevitte. 2006. "Do Polls Influence the Vote?" In *Capturing Campaign Effects*, Richard G. C. Johnston and Henry E. Brady, eds., 263–279. Ann Arbor: University of Michigan Press.

Blumer, Herbert. 1958. "Race Prejudice as a Sense of Group Position." *Pacific Sociological Review* 9 (1): 3–7.

Bobo, Lawrence D. 1988. "Group Conflict, Prejudice, and the Paradox of Contemporary Racial Attitudes." In *Eliminating Racism: Profiles in Controversy*, Phyllis A. Katz and Dalmas A. Taylor, eds., 85–114. New York: Plenum Press.

———. 1999. "Prejudice as Group Position: Microfoundations of a Sociological Approach to Racism and Race Relations." *Journal of Social Issues* 55 (3): 445–472.

Bobo, Lawrence, and Vincent L. Hutchings. 1996. "Perceptions of Racial Group Competition: Extending Blumer's Theory of Group Position to a Multiracial Social Context." *American Sociological Review* 61 (6): 951–972.

Bobo, Lawrence D., James R. Kluegel, and Ryan A. Smith. 1997. "Laissez-Faire Racism: The Crystallization of a Kinder, Gentler, Antiblack Ideology." In *Racial Attitudes in the 1990s: Continuity and Change*, Steven A. Tuch and Jack K. Martin, eds., 15–44. Westport, Conn.: Praeger.

Bonczar, Thomas P. 2003. "Prevalence of Imprisonment in the U.S. Population, 1974–2001." USDOJ Office of Justice Programs. http: //bjs.ojp.usdoj.gov.

Bowen, William G., and Derek Bok. 2000. *The Shape of the River: Long-Term Consequences of Considering Race in College and University Admissions*. Princeton, N.J.: Princeton University Press.

Bowler, Shaun, Todd Donovan, and David Brockington. 2003. *Electoral Reform and Minority Representation*. Columbus: Ohio State University Press.

Brader, Ted, Nicholas A. Valentino, and Elizabeth Suhay. 2008. "What Triggers Public Opposition to Immigration? Anxiety, Group Cues, and Immigration Threat." *American Journal of Political Science* 52 (4): 959–978.

Branch, Taylor. 1988. *Parting the Waters: America in the King Years, 1954-63*. New York: Simon and Schuster.

Brewer, Marilynn B. 1988. "A Dual-Process Model of Impression Formation." In *Advances in Social Cognition*, T. K. Srull and R. S. Wyereds, eds., 1–36. Hillsdale, N.J.: Erlbaum.

Brewer, Paul R., and Clyde Wilcox. 2005. "Same-Sex Marriage and Civil Unions." *Public Opinion Quarterly* 69 (4): 599–616.

Britz, Jennifer Delahunty. 2006. "To All the Girls I've Rejected." *New York Times*, March 23.

Brophy, Alfred L. 2001. "Assessing State and City Culpability: The Riot and the Law." In *Tulsa Race Riot: A Report by the Oklahoma Commission to Study the Tulsa Race Riot of 1921*, 153–174. http: //www.okhistory.org.

———. 2002. *Deconstructing the Dreamland: The Tulsa Riot of 1921*. Oxford: Oxford University Press.

Bullock, John G. 2011. "Elite Influence on Public Opinion in an Informed Electorate." *American Political Science Review* 105 (3): 496–515.

Burdman, Pamela. 1999. "UC Regents to Approve 4% Admissions Policy; Top Seniors From Each School Would Be Accepted." *San Francisco Chronicle*, March 19.

Burstein, Paul. 1979. "Public Opinion, Demonstrations, and the Passage of Antidiscrimination Legislation." *Public Opinion Quarterly* 43: 157–172.

Butler, Daniel M., and David E. Broockman. 2011. "Do Politicians Racially Discriminate Against Constituents? A Field Experiment on State Legislators." *American Journal of Political Science* 55 (3): 463–477.

Campbell, Angus, Philip E. Converse, Warren E. Miller, and Donald E. Stokes. 1960. *The American Voter*. Chicago: University of Chicago Press.

Carsey, Thomas M. 1995. "The Contextual Effects of Race on White Voter Behavior: The 1989 New York City Mayoral Election." *Journal of Politics* 57: 221–228.

Cataldo, Everett F., and John D. Holm. 1983. "Voting on School Finances: A Test of Competing Theories." *Western Political Quarterly* 36: 619–631.

Charleston Post and Courier. 1999. "Beasley: No NAACP Support." November 27, p. B1.

Cole, David. 1999. *No Equal Justice: Race and Class in the American Criminal Justice System*. New York: New Press.

Converse, Philip E. 1964. "The Nature of Belief Systems in Mass Publics." In *Ideology and Discontent*, David E. Apter, ed. New York: Free Press, 206–261.

Converse, Philip E. 1970. "Attitudes and Nonattitudes: Continuation of a Dialogue." In *Quantitative Analysis of Social Problems*, ed. Edward R Tufte. Reading, Mass.: Addison-Wesley, 168–189.

Cook, S. W., and A. C. Welch. 1940. "Methods of Measuring the Practical Effect of Polls on Public Opinion." *Journal of Applied Psychology* 23: 441–454.

Cosmides, Leda, and John Tooby. 1994. "Better than Rational: Evolutionary Psychology and the Invisible Hand." *American Economic Review* 84 (2): 327–332.

Cronon, E. David. 1969. *Black Moses: The Story of Marcus Garvey and the Universal Negro Improvement Association*. Madison: University of Wisconsin Press.

Crosby, Faye J., and Diana I. Cordova. 1996. "Words Worth of Wisdom: Toward an Understanding of Affirmative Action." *Journal of Social Issues* 52: 33–49.

Crowder, Kyle, and Scott J. South. 2008. "Spatial Dynamics of White Flight: The Effects of Local and Extralocal Racial Conditions on Neighborhood Out-Migration." *American Sociological Review* 73 (5): 792–812.

Cullen, Julie Berry, Mark C. Long, and Randall Reback. 2011. "Jockeying for Position: Strategic High School Choice Under Texas' Top Ten Percent Plan." *NBER Working Paper Series* 16663. http: //www.nber.org.

Dahl, Robert A. 1967. *Pluralist Democracy in the United States*. Chicago: Rand McNally & Company.

Darcy, R. 1986. "Position Effects with Party Column Ballots." *Western Political Quarterly* 39: 648–661.

Davenport, Jim. 2000. "Hodges Signs Act Removing Confederate Flag from State-house Dome." *Associated Press*, May 24.

Davis, Gray. 1999. Inaugural Address, January 4. http: //governors.library.ca.gov.

Davis, Michelle R. 1999. "S.C. Boycott Is Ratified by NAACP." *Charleston Post and Courier*, October 17, p. 1.

Dawson, Michael C., and Rovana Popoff. 2004. "Reparations: Justice and Greed in Black and White." *Du Bois Review* 1 (1): 47–91.

Druckman, James N. 2004. "Political Preference Formation: Competition, Delibera-tion, and the (Ir)relevance of Framing Effects." *American Political Science Review* 98 (4): 671–686.

———. 2005. "Does Political Information Matter?" *Political Communication* 22: 515–519.

Druckman, James N., Donald P. Green, James H. Kuklinski, and Arthur Lupia. 2006. "The Growth and Development of Experimental Research in Political Science." *American Political Science Review* 100 (4): 627–635.

Druckman, James N., Donald P. Green, James H. Kuklinski, and Arthur Lupia. 2011. "Experimentation in Political Science." In *Cambridge Handbook of Experimental Political Science*, James N. Druckman et al., eds., 3–14. New York: Cambridge University Press.

———, eds. 2011. *Cambridge Handbook of Experimental Political Science*. New York: Cambridge University Press.

Druckman, James N., and Arthur Lupia. 2008. "Preference Formation." *Annual Re-view of Political Science* 3: 1–24.

Duncan, Greg J., Johanne Boisjoly, Dan M. Levy, Michael Kremer, and Jacque Eccles. 2003. "Empathy or Antipathy? The Consequences of Racially and Socially Diverse Peers on Attitudes and Behaviors." Working Paper, Institute for Policy Research, Northwestern University, Chicago. http: //www.ipr.northwestern.edu.

Dunne, Stephanie, W. Robert Reed, and James Wilbanks. 1997. "Endogenizing the Median Voter: Public Choice Goes to School." *Public Choice* 93: 99–118.

Durr, Robert H., John B. Gilmour, and Christina Wolbrecht. 1997. "Explaining Con-gressional Approval." *American Journal of Political Science* 41: 175–207.

Dutton, Donald G., and Arthur P. Aron. 1974. "Some Evidence for Heightened Sexual Attraction Under Conditions of High Anxiety." *Journal of Personality and Social Psychology* 30 (4): 510–517.

Edsall, Thomas B., and Mary D. Edsall. 1991. *Chain Reaction: The Impact of Race, Rights, and Taxes on American Politics*. New York: W. W. Norton.

Ellsworth, Scott. 2001. "The Tulsa Race Riot." In *Tulsa Race Riot: A Report by the Okla-homa Commission to Study the Tulsa Race Riot of 1921*, 37–102. http: //www.okhis tory.org.

Espenshade, Thomas J., Chang Y. Chung, and Joan L. Walling. 2004. "Admissions Pref-erences for Minority Students, Athletes, and Legacies at Elite Universities." *Social Science Quarterly* 85: 1422–1447.

Evans, O. 1963. "OK Accord with City, Deny Bias." *Philadelphia Bulletin*, August 20.

FBI Uniform Crime Reporting Program. *Hate Crimes Statistics* (1996–2000). http://www.fbi.gov.

Fallow, Michael. 2005. "A Sorry State of Affairs." *Southland (New Zealand) Times*, February 26.

Farber, Jim. 2008. "Geraldine Ferraro Lets Her Emotions Do the Talking." *Daily Breeze*, March 7. http://www.dailybreeze.com.

Fazio, Russell H., and Michael A. Olson. 2003. "Implicit Measures in Social Cognition Research: Their Meaning and Use." *Annual Review of Psychology* 54 (1): 297–327.

Fears, Darryl. 2005. "Seeking More Than Apologies for Slavery." *Washington Post*, June 20.

Finkelman, Paul. 2001. *Slavery and the Founders*. Armonk, N.Y.: M. E. Sharpe.

Fiorina, Morris P., and Samuel J. Abrams. 2008. "Political Polarization in the American Public." *Annual Review of Political Science* 11 (1): 563–588.

Fossett, Mark A., and Jill A. Kiecult. 1989. "The Relative Size of Minority Populations and White Racial Attitudes." *Social Science Quarterly* 70 (4): 820–835.

Franklin, John Hope, and Scott Ellsworth. 2001. "History Knows No Fences: An Overview." In *Tulsa Race Riot: A Report by the Oklahoma Commission to Study the Tulsa Race Riot of 1921*, 21–36. http://www.okhistory.org.

Franklin, John Hope, and Alfred A. Moss Jr. 1994. *From Slavery to Freedom: A History of Negro Americans*, 7th ed. New York: McGraw-Hill.

Freedman, David A. 2008. "On Regression Adjustments to Experimental Data." *Advances in Applied Mathematics* 40 (2): 180–193.

Gaines, Brian J., James H. Kuklinski, and Paul J. Quirk. 2006. "The Logic of the Survey Experiment Reexamined." *Political Analysis* 15 (1): 1–20.

Gallup. 2008. "Clinton Now at 47 Percent to Obama's 45 Percent." *Gallup Daily*. http://www.gallup.com.

Gallup. 2009. "State of the States." http://www.gallup.com/poll/125066/State-States.aspx.

Gamson, William A., and Andre Modigliani. 1987. "The Changing Culture of Affirmative Action." In *Research in Political Sociology*, Richard G. Braungart, ed. Greenwich, Conn.: JAI Press.

Gay, Claudine. 2002. "Spirals of Trust? The Effect of Descriptive Representation Between Citizens and their Government." *American Journal of Political Science* 46 (4): 717–733.

Gerber, Elisabeth R., and Rebecca B. Morton. 1998. "Primary Election Systems and Representation." *Journal of Law, Economics, and Organization* 14 (2): 304–324.

Gerber, Elisabeth R., Rebecca B. Morton, and Thomas A. Rietz. 1998. "Minority Representation in Multimember Districts." *American Political Science Review* 92 (1): 127–144.

Gerbner, Katharine. 2007. "'We Are Against the Traffik of Men-Body': The Germantown Quaker Protest of 1688 and the Origins of American Abolitionism." *Pennsylvania History* 74 (2): 149–172.

Gibson, James L. 1998. "A Sober Second Thought: An Experiment in Persuading Russians to Tolerate." *American Journal of Political Science* 42 (3): 819–850.

Gilens, Martin. 2001. "Political Ignorance and Collective Policy Preferences." *American Political Science Review* 95: 379–396.

Giles, Micheal W. 1977. "Percent Black and Racial Hostility: An Old Assumption Reexamined." *Social Science Quarterly* 58: 412–417.

Giles, Micheal W., Douglas S. Gatlin, and Everett F. Cataldo. 1976. "Parental Support for School Referenda." *Journal of Politics* 38: 442–451.

Giles, Micheal W., and Kaenan Hertz. 1994. "Racial Threat and Partisan Identification." *American Political Science Review* 88: 317–326.

Gilovich, Thomas, Victoria Husted Medvec, and Daniel Kahneman. 1998. "Varieties of Regret: A Debate and Partial Resolution." *Psychological Review* 105 (3): 602–605.

Ginges, Jeremy, Scott Atran, Douglas Medin, and Khalil Shikaki. 2007. "Sacred Bounds on Rational Resolution of Violent Political Conflict." *Proceedings of the National Academic of Sciences* 104 (18): 7357–7360.

Glaser, James M. 1994. "Back to the Black Belt: Racial Environment and White Racial Attitudes in the South." *Journal of Politics* 56: 21–41.

———. 2001. "The Preference Puzzle: Educational Differences in Racial-Political Attitudes." *Political Behavior* 23: 313–334.

———. 2002. "White Voters, Black Schools: Structuring Racial Choices with a Checklist Ballot." *American Journal of Political Science* 46: 35–46.

———. 2003. "Social Context and Inter-Group Political Attitudes: Experiments in Group Conflict Theory." *British Journal of Political Science* 33 (4): 607–620.

———. 2006. "Public Support for Political Compromise on a Volatile Racial Issue: Insight from the Survey Experiment." *Political Psychology* 27: 423–439.

Glazer, Nathan. 1983. *Ethnic Dilemmas, 1964–1982.* Cambridge, Mass.: Harvard University Press.

Goble, Danny. 2001. "Final Report of the Oklahoma Commission to Study the Tulsa Race Riot of 1921." In *Tulsa Race Riot: A Report by the Oklahoma Commission to Study the Tulsa Race Riot of 1921,* 1–20. http: //www.okhistory.org.

Graham, Jesse, Jonathan Haidt, and Brian A. Nosek. 2009. "Liberals and Conservatives Rely on Different Sets of Moral Foundations." *Journal of Personality and Social Psychology* 96 (5): 1029–1046.

Green, Donald Philip. 1992. "The Price Elasticity of Mass Preferences." *American Political Science Review* 86 (1): 128–148.

Green, Donald P., and Janelle S. Wong. 2009. "Tolerance and the Contact Hypothesis: A Field Experiment." In *The Political Psychology of Democratic Citizenship,* Eugene Borgida, Christopher M. Federico, and John L. Sullivan, eds., 228–246. New York: Oxford University Press.

Greenhouse, Linda. 2003. "The Supreme Court: The Justices; Context and the Court." *New York Times,* June 24.

Greenwald, Anthony G., T. Andrew Poehlman, Eric Luis Uhlmann, and Mahzarin R. Banaji. 2009. "Understanding and Using the Implicit Association Test: III. Meta-Analysis of Predictive Validity." *Journal of Personality and Social Psychology* 97 (1): 17–41.

Grodsky, Eric, and Demetra Kalogrides. 2008. "The Declining Significance of Race in College Admissions Decisions." *American Journal of Education* 115 (1): 1–33.

Haidt, Jonathan. 2012. *The Righteous Mind: Why Good People Are Divided by Politics and Religion.* New York: Pantheon.

Hainmueller, Jens, and Michael J. Hiscox. 2010. "Attitudes Toward Highly Skilled and Low-Skilled Immigration: Evidence from a Survey Experiment." *American Political Science Review* 104 (1): 61–84.

Hajnal, Zoltan L. 2009. "Who Loses in American Democracy? A Count of Votes Demonstrates the Limited Representation of African Americans." *American Political Science Review* 103 (1): 37–57.

Hall, John Stuart, and Philip K. Piele. 1976. "Selected Determinants of Precinct Voting Decisions in School Budget Elections." *Western Political Quarterly* 29: 440–456.

Hamilton, James T., and Helen F. Ladd. 1996. "Biased Ballots: The Impact of Ballot Structure on North Carolina Elections in 1992." *Public Choice* 87: 259–280.

Harris, John F. 1999. "Clinton 'Concerned' on Police Conduct; More Funding Sought for Ethics Training, Minority Recruitment." *Washington Post*, March 14.

Harrison, David A., David M. Mayer, Lisa M. Leslie, David A. Kravitz, and Dalit Lev-Arey. 2006. "Understanding Attitudes Toward Affirmative Action Programs in Employment: Summary and Meta-Analysis of 35 Years of Research." *Journal of Applied Psychology* 91: 1013–1036.

Hayden, Cathy. 1991. "Bond Issue Campaign Uses Creativity, Much Hard Work." *Jackson Clarion-Ledger*, June 2.

Heckman, James J., and Alan B. Krueger. 2004. *Inequality in America: What Role for Human Capital Policies?* Cambridge, Mass.: MIT Press.

Heilprin, John. 1997. "Flag Flap Greets Lawmakers." *Charleston Post and Courier*, January 15, p. A1.

Hewstone, Miles, Alexander Hantzi, and Lucy Johnston. 1991. "Social Categorization and Person Memory: The Pervasiveness of Race as an Organizing Principle." *European Journal of Social Psychology* 21 (6): 517–528.

Hibbing, John R., and Elizabeth Theiss-Morse. 1995. *Congress as Public Enemy: Public Attitudes Toward American Political Institutions.* Cambridge: Cambridge University Press.

———. 2001. "Process Preferences and American Politics: What the People Want Government to Be." *American Political Science Review* 95: 145–153.

Highton, Benjamin, and Raymond E. Wolfinger. 1992. "Estimating the Size of Minority Groups." Memorandum written to the Board of Overseers of the National Election Studies, January 24.

Hirsch, Arnold R. 1983. *Making the Second Ghetto: Race and Housing in Chicago, 1940–1960*. Cambridge: Cambridge University Press.

Hirsch, James S. 2002. *Riot and Remembrance: The Tulsa Race War and Its Legacy*. Boston: Houghton Mifflin.

Hochschild, Jennifer L. 1986. *What's Fair: American Beliefs about Distributive Justice*. Cambridge, Mass.: Harvard University Press.

Holland, Paul. 1986. "Statistics and Causal Inference." *Journal of the American Statistical Association* 81 (396): 945–960.

Hyman, Herbert H., and Paul B. Sheatsley. 1950. "The Current Status of American Public Opinion." In *The Teaching of Contemporary Affairs*, J. C. Payne, ed., 11–34. Washington, D.C.: National Council for the Social Studies.

Iceland, John, Daniel H. Weinberg, and Erika Steinmetz. 2002. "Racial and Ethnic Residential Segregation in the United States: 1980–2000." U.S. Census. http: // www.census.gov/hhes/www/housing/housing_patterns/pdf/censr-3.pdf.

Ioannidis, John P. A. 2005. "Why Most Published Research Findings Are False." *PLOS Medicine* 2 (8): 696–701.

Jacoby, William G. 2000. "Issue Framing and Public Opinion on Government Spending." *American Journal of Political Science* 44: 750–767.

Jaschik, Scott. 2008. "Need Blind, but 'Gapping.'" *Inside Higher Ed*, November 26. http: //www.insidehighered.com.

Jefferson, Thomas. 1788 [1904]. "To Jean Pierre Brissot de Warville." In *The Works of Thomas Jefferson, vol. 5 (Correspondence 1786–1789)*, Federal Edition (New York: G. P. Putnam and Sons). http: //oll.libertyfund.org/title/802/86695.

Johnson, Wayne C. 1998. "Defeating Proposition 223: How Opponents of the '95/5' School Funding Initiative Dramatically Turned Around Public Opinion to Beat It 55–45." *Campaigns and Elections* 19 (10): 38–41.

Jordan, Hallye. 1999. "Davis Vetoes Bill Allowing Outreach; Governor Says Measure Would Violate Ban on Affirmative Action." *San Jose Mercury News*, July 29.

Kahneman, Daniel, and Amos Tversky. 1984. "Choices, Values, and Frames." *American Psychologist* 39: 341–350.

Kane, Thomas J. 1998. "Misconceptions in the Debate over Affirmative Action." In *Chilling Admissions: The Affirmative Action Crisis and the Search for Alternatives*, Gary Orfield and Edward Miller, eds., 17–31. Cambridge, Mass.: Harvard Education Publishing Group.

———2003. "The Long Road to Race-Blindness." *Science* 302 (5645): 571–573.

Katznelson, Ira. 2006. *When Affirmative Action Was White: An Untold History of Racial Inequality in Twentieth-Century America*. New York: W. W. Norton.

Kenney, Patrick J., and Tom W. Rice. 1994. "The Psychology of Political Momentum." *Political Research Quarterly* 47 (4): 923–938.

Key, V. O. 1949. *Southern Politics in State and Nation*. Knoxville: University of Tennessee Press.

Kinder, Donald R. Forthcoming. "Prejudice and Politics." In *The Oxford Handbook of Political Psychology, Second Edition*, Leonie Huddy, David O Sears, and Jack Levy, eds. New York: Oxford University Press.

Kinder, Donald R. 1998. "Opinion and Action in the Realm of Politics." In *Handbook of Social Psychology*, Daniel Gilbert, Susan Fiske, and G. Linzey, eds., 778–867. New York: McGraw-Hill.

Kinder, Donald R., and Allison Dale-Riddle. 2011. *The End of Race? Obama, 2008, and Racial Politics in America*. New Haven, Conn.: Yale University Press.

Kinder, Donald R., and Katherine W. Drake. 2009. "Myrdal's Prediction." *Political Psychology* 30 (4): 1–30.

Kinder, Donald R., and Tali Mendelberg. 1995. "Cracks in American Apartheid: The Political Impact of Prejudice Among Desegregated Whites." *Journal of Politics* 57: 402–424.

Kinder, Donald R., and Lynn M. Sanders. 1996. *Divided by Color: Racial Politics and Democratic Ideals*. Chicago: University of Chicago Press.

Klinkner, Philip A., and Rogers M. Smith. 1999. *The Unsteady March: The Rise and Decline of Racial Equality in America*. Chicago: University of Chicago Press.

Kochhar, Rakesh, Richard Fry, and Paul Taylor. 2011. "Wealth Gaps Rise to Record Highs Between Whites, Blacks and Hispanics." Pew Research Center. http: //pew socialtrends.org.

Kozol, Jonathan. 2005. "Still Separate, Still Unequal: America's Educational Apartheid." *Harper's Magazine* 311 (1864): 40–54.

Krehbiel, Randy. 2000. "Riot Panel Votes for Reparations. Legislators on Commission Say Proposal Doomed to Rejection." *Tulsa World*, February 5.

———. 2002. "Checks in the Mail After 80 Years; Compensation of $28,000 Paid to 131 Survivors of 1921 Conflict." *Tulsa World*, April 9.

Kuklinski, James H., Paul M. Sniderman, Kathleen Knight, Thomas Piazza, Philip E. Tetlock, Gordon R. Lawrence, and Barbara Mellers. 1997. "Racial Prejudice and Attitudes Toward Affirmative Action." *American Journal of Political Science* 41: 402–419.

Kurzban, Robert, and C. Athena Aktipis. 2007. "Modularity and the Social Mind: Are Psychologists Too Selfish?" *Personality and Social Psychology Review* 11: 131–149.

Kurzban, Robert, John Tooby, and Leda Cosmides. 2001. "Can Race be Erased? Coalitional Computation and Social Categorization." *Proceedings of the National Academy of Science* 98 (26): 15387–15392.

Lacy, Dean. 2001. "Nonseparable Preferences in Survey Responses." *American Journal of Political Science* 45: 239–258.

Larson, Jessica, and Stephen Menendian. 2008. "Anti-Affirmative Action Ballot Initiatives." Report by the Kirwan Institute for the Study of Race and Ethnicity, Ohio State University (December).

Lasswell, Harold D. 1950. *Politics: Who Gets What, When, How*. New York: P. Smith.

Lazare, Aaron. 1995. "Go Ahead, Say You're Sorry." *Psychology Today* 28 (1): 41–43, 76–78.

———. 2004. *On Apology*. New York: Oxford University Press.

Lemann, Nicholas. 1991. *The Promised Land: The Great Black Migration and How It Changed America*. New York: Alfred A. Knopf.

Levey, Curt A. 2003. "Colleges Should Take No Comfort in the Supreme Court's Reprieve." *Chronicle of Higher Education*, July 18.

Lin, Ann Chih, and David R. Harris. 2009. "The Colors of Poverty: Why Racial and Ethnic Disparities Persist." National Poverty Center Policy Briefs Series. http: // www.npc.umich.edu.

Lupia, Arthur. 1994. "Shortcuts Versus Encyclopedias: Information and Voting Behavior in California Insurance Reform Elections." *American Political Science Review* 88 (1): 63–76.

Lupia, Arthur, and Richard Johnston. 2001. "Are Voters to Blame? Voter Competence and Elite Maneuvers in Public Referendums." In *Referendum Democracy: Citizens, Elites, and Deliberation in Referendum Campaigns*, Matthew Mendelsohn and Andrew Parkin, eds., 191–210. Hampshire, England: Palgrave.

Madigan, Tim. 2001. *The Burning: Massacre, Destruction, and the Tulsa Race Riot of 1921*. New York: Thomas Dunne Books.

Manning, Jennifer E., and Colleen J. Shogan. 2011. "African American Members of the United States Congress: 1870–2011." Congressional Research Service. http:// www.senate.gov.

Marks, Carole. 1989. *Farewell—We're Good and Gone: The Great Black Migration*. Bloomington: Indiana University Press.

McCarty, Nolan, Keith T. Poole, and Howard Rosenthal. 2008. *Polarized America: The Dance of Ideology and Unequal Riches*. Cambridge, Mass.: MIT Press.

McGraw, Seamus. 1999. "Ouster Follows His Remarks on a Racial Issue." *(Bergen County) Record*, March 1.

McKenzie, Brian D. 2011. "Barack Obama, Jeremiah Wright, and Public Opinion in the 2008 Presidential Primaries." *Political Psychology* 32 (6): 943–961.

McVeigh, Rory. 2009. *The Rise of the Ku Klux Klan: Right-Wing Movements and National Politics*. Minneapolis: University of Minnesota Press.

Mehrabian, Albert. 1998. "Effects of Poll Reports on Voter Preferences." *Journal of Applied Social Psychology* 28 (23): 2119–2130.

Mellers, Barbara, Ralph Hertwig, and Daniel Kahneman. 2001. "Do Frequency Representations Eliminate Conjunction Effects? An Exercise in Adversarial Collaboration." *Psychological Science* 12 (4): 269–275.

Merida, Devin. 1995. "Gingrich Offers Provocative Views on Racial Issues; Speaker Suggests Money Misspent on Busing, Says 'Habits of Acquisition' Could Aid Poor Blacks." *Washington Post*, June 16.

Miller, Joanne M., and Jon A. Krosnick. 1998. "The Impact of Candidate Name Order on Election Outcomes." *Public Opinion Quarterly* 62: 291–330.

Minow, Martha. 1998. *Between Vengeance and Forgiveness: Facing History*. New York: Beacon Press.

Mississippi Department of Education. "Mississippi Assessment and Accountability Reporting System." http: //orsap.mde.k12.ms.us/MAARS/index.jsp.

Moreland, Laurence W., and Robert P. Steed. 1997. "South Carolina: Elephants Stroll Through the Palmettos." In *The 1996 Presidential Election in the South: Southern Party Systems in the 1990s*, Laurence W. Moreland and Robert P. Steed, eds., 111–130. Westport, Conn.: Praeger.

Mueller, John E. 1969. "Voting on the Propositions: Ballot Patterns and Historical Trends in California." *American Political Science Review* 63: 1197–1212.

Mutz, Diana C. 1997. "Mechanisms of Momentum: Does Thinking Make It So?" *Journal of Politics* 59 (1): 104–125.

———. 2002. "Cross-Cutting Social Networks: Testing Democratic Theory in Practice." *American Political Science Review* 96 (1): 111–126.

———. 2011. *Population-Based Survey Experiments*. Princeton, N.J.: Princeton University Press.

Mutz, Diana C., and Byron Reeves. 2005. "The New Videomalaise: Effects of Televised Incivility on Political Trust." *American Political Science Review* 99 (1): 1–15.

Nadeau, Richard, Richard G. Niemi, and Jeffrey Levine. 1993. "Innumeracy About Minority Populations." *Public Opinion Quarterly* 57: 33–47.

Nagourney, Adam. 2008. "Racial Barrier Falls in Decisive Victory." *New York Times*, November 5, p. A1.

National Center for Education Statistics. 2006. *United States High School Sophomores: A Twenty-Two Year Comparison, 1990–2002. Statistical Analysis Report*. NCES-2006-327. Washington, D.C.: U.S. Department of Education, National Center for Education Statistics.

National Conference of State Legislatures. 2009. "African American Legislators, 2009." http: //www.ncsl.org.

Nelson, Melissa. 1999. "Panel Debates Riot Reparations." *Daily Oklahoman*. November 23.

Nelson, W. Dale. 1988. "Payment to Interned Japanese-Americans Gets Reagan's OK." *Associated Press*. August 10. http: //www.apnewsarchive.com/

New York Times. 1964. "Student Grants Set in Mississippi." July 16.

New York Times. 1999a. "Panel Seeks Clearer View of the 1921 Tulsa Race Riot." February 21.

———. 1999b. "Views on State Police Sharply Divided by Race." April 2.

———. 2000. "Excerpts from McCain's Remarks on Confederate Flag." April 20.

Newport, Frank. 2011. "For First Time, Majority of Americans Favor Gay Marriage." *Gallup Politics*. May 20. http: //www.gallup.com.

Newsweek Poll. 2003. Conducted by Princeton Survey Research Associates. Princeton, N.J. January 18.

Newton-Small, Jay. 2008. "Reaction to the Obama Speech." *Time*, March 18.

Nisbett, Richard E., and Timothy DeCamp Wilson. 1977. "Telling More Than We Can Know: Verbal Reports on Mental Processes." *Psychological Review* 84: 231–253.

Nobles, Melissa. 2008. *The Politics of Official Apologies*. Cambridge: Cambridge University Press.

Noelle-Neumann, Elisabeth. 1984. *The Spiral of Silence: Public Opinion, Our Social Skin*. Chicago: University of Chicago Press.

Noonan, Peggy. 2008. "A Thinking Man's Speech." *Wall Street Journal*, March 22, p. W16.

O'Connor, Colleen. 2004. "Who's Sorry Now? An Orgy of Apologies Spreading Across the World." *Denver Post*, April 15, p. L1.

Oliver, J. Eric, and Tali Mendelberg. 2000. "Reconsidering the Environmental Determinants of White Racial Attitudes." *American Journal of Political Science* 44: 574–589.

Orfield, Gary, and Chungmei Lee. 2007. "Historic Reversals, Accelerating Resegregation, and the Need for New Integration Strategies." Civil Rights Project, UCLA. http: // civilrightsproject.ucla.edu.

Oskamp, Stuart, ed. 2000. *Reducing Prejudice and Discrimination*. Washington, D.C.: Psychology Press.

Paluck, Elizabeth Levy, and Donald P. Green. 2009. "Prejudice Reduction: What Works? A Review and Assessment of Research and Practice." *Annual Review of Psychology* 60: 339–367.

Panagopoulos, Costas, and Donald P. Green. 2008. "Field Experiments Testing the Impact of Radio Advertisements on Electoral Competition." *American Journal of Political Science* 52 (1): 156–168.

Parker, Jocelyn. 2003. "Michigan Businesses Pleased with Supreme Court Decision." *Detroit Free Press*, June 24.

Pasek, Josh, et al. 2009. "Determinants of Turnout and Candidate Choice in the 2008 U.S. Presidential Election." *Public Opinion Quarterly* 73: 943–994.

Payne, B. Keith, Clara Michelle Cheng, Olesya Govorun, and Brandon D. Stewart. 2005. "An Inkblot for Attitudes: Affect Misattribution as Implicit Measurement." *Journal of Personality and Social Psy*chology 89 (3): 277–293.

Payne, B. Keith, Jon A. Krosnick, Josh Pasek, Yptach Lelkes, Omair Akhtar, and Trevor Tompson. 2010. "Implicit and Explicit Prejudice in the 2008 Presidential Election." *Journal of Experimental Social Psychology* 46: 367–374.

Pettigrew, Thomas F., and Linda R. Tropp. 2006. "A Meta-Analytic Test of Intergroup Contact Theory." *Journal of Personality and Social Psychology* 90 (5): 751–783.

Phi Delta Kappan. 1984–1994. "Annual Gallup Poll of the Public's Attitudes Toward the Public Schools." Published annually in the September issue.

Platt, John R. 1964. "Strong Inference." *Science* 146 (3642): 347–353.

Plouffe, David. 2008. *The Audacity to Win: The Inside Story and Lessons of Barack Obama's Historic Victory*. New York: Viking Adult.

Popper, Karl. (1959) 2010. *The Logic of Scientific Discovery*. New York: Routledge Classics.

Porter, Nicole D. 2010. "Expanding the Vote: State Felony Disenfranchisement Reform, 1997–2010." The Sentencing Project. http: //www.sentencingproject.org.

Presser, Stanley, and Howard Schuman. 1980. "The Measurement of a Middle Position in Attitude Surveys." *Public Opinion Quarterly* 44: 70–85.

Preston, Jennifer. 1999. "Trooper Says State Police in New Jersey Discriminate." *New York Times*, February 6.

Provine, Doris Marie. 2007. *Unequal Under Law: Race in the War on Drugs.* Chicago: University of Chicago Press.

Rasinski, Kenneth A. 1981. "The Effect of Question Wording on Public Support for Government Spending." *Public Opinion Quarterly* 53 (3): 388–394.

Reed, John Shelton. 1972. *The Enduring South: Subcultural Persistence in Mass Society.* Chapel Hill: University of North Carolina Press.

Reeves, Keith. 1997. *Voting Hopes or Fears? White Voters, Black Candidates and Racial Politics in America.* New York: Oxford University Press.

Remnick, David. 2008. "The Joshua Generation." *New Yorker*, November 17, pp. 68–83.

Richardson, John D. 2005. "Switching Social Identities: The Influence of Editorial Framing on Reader Attitudes Toward Affirmative Action and African Americans." *Communication Research* 32: 503–528.

Riker, William H. 1986. *The Art of Political Manipulation.* New Haven, Conn.: Yale University Press.

———. 1988. *Liberalism Against Populism.* Long Grove, Ill.: Waveland Press, Inc.

Roche, Declan. 2003. *Accountability in Restorative Justice.* Oxford: Oxford University Press.

Romano, Lois. 2000. "Tulsa Airs a Race Riot's Legacy; State Historical Panel's Call for Restitution Spurs a Debate." *Washington Post*, January 19.

Rosin, Hanna. 2010. "The End of Men." *Atlantic*, July–August.

Rosovsky, Henry. 1990. *The University: An Owner's Manual.* New York: W. W. Norton.

Ross, Brian. 2008. "Obama's Pastor: God Damn America, U.S. to Blame for 9/11." *ABC News.com*, March 13.

Ross, Lee, and Richard E. Nisbett. 1991. *The Person and the Situation: Perspectives of Social Psychology.* New York: McGraw Hill-College.

Ryan, Timothy J., and Kristyn L. Miller-Karl. 2011. "Stereotypes and Stereotype Revision: When Do Candidate Traits Affect Voters' Perceptions?" Paper presented at the 2011 meeting of the Midwest Political Science Association, Chicago.

Sander, Richard H. and Stuart Taylor. 2012. *Mismatch: How Affirmative Action Hurts Students It's Intended to Help.* New York: Basic Books.

Savage, David G. 2003. "Bush's Opposition to Racial Preferences Gets Big Support." *Los Angeles Times*, February 6.

Schuman, Howard, Charlotte Steeh, Lawrence D. Bobo, and Maria Krysan. 1998. *Racial Attitudes in America: Trends and Interpretations*, revised ed. Cambridge, Mass.: Harvard University Press.

Sears, David O., and Jack Citrin. 1982. *Tax Revolt: Something for Nothing in California.* Cambridge, Mass.: Harvard University Press.

Sears, David O., Richard Lau, Tom Tyler, and Harris M. Allen Jr. 1980. "Self-Interest vs. Symbolic Politics in Policy Attitudes and Presidential Voting." *American Political Science Review* 74 (3): 670–684.

Seelye, Katherine Q. 2008. "Ferraro's Obama Remarks Become Talk of Campaign." *New York Times*, March 12.

Shapiro, Thomas M. 2004. *The Hidden Cost of Being African American: How Wealth Perpetuates Inequality.* New York: Oxford University Press.

Sharp, Elaine B. 1987. "Voting on Citywide Propositions—Further Tests of Competing Explanations." *Urban Affairs Review* 23: 233–248.

Sherif, Muzafer. 1956. "Experiments in Group Conflict." *Scientific American* 195: 54–58.

Sidanius, Jim, Pam Singh, John J. Hetts, and Chris Federico. 2000. "It's Not Affirmative Action, It's the Blacks." In *Racialized Politics: The Debate About Racism in America*, David O. Sears, Jim Sidanius, and Lawrence Bobo, eds., 191–235. Chicago: University of Chicago Press.

Simmons, Lee. 1999. "Effect of NAACP's Planned Tourism Boycott Debated." *Rock Hill Herald*, July 17, p. 1A.

Slevin, Peter. 2006. "Court Battle Likely on Affirmative Action; Michigan Voters Approved Ban, but Opponents of the Measure Persist." *Washington Post*, November 18.

Smith, A. Wade. 1981. "Racial Tolerance as a Function of Group Position." *American Sociological Review* 46 (5): 558–573.

Smith, Steven S., Jason M. Roberts, and Ryan J. Vander Wielen. 2006. *The American Congress.* Oxford: Oxford University Press.

Sniderman, Paul M., and Edward G. Carmines. 1997. *Reaching Beyond Race.* Cambridge, Mass.: Harvard University Press.

Sniderman, Paul M., and Thomas Piazza. 1993. *The Scar of Race.* Cambridge, Mass.: Belknap Press of Harvard University Press.

Sniderman, Paul M., and Philip E. Tetlock. 1986. "Symbolic Racism: Problems of Motive Attribution in Political Analysis." *Journal of Social Issues* 42 (2): 129–150.

Sniderman, Paul M., and Sean M. Theriault. 2004. "The Structure of Political Argument and the Logic of Issue Framing." In *Studies in Public Opinion*, William E. Saris and Paul M. Sniderman, eds., 133–165. Princeton, N.J.: Princeton University Press.

Southern Focus Poll. 1998. Conducted by the Institute for Research in Social Science. Chapel Hill, North Carolina, Spring 1998. http://www.irss.unc.edu.

Sowell, Thomas. 2005. "Affirmative Action in the United States." In *Affirmative Action Around the World: An Empirical Study.* New Haven, Conn.: Yale University Press.

Stangor, Charles, Laure Lynch, Changming Duan, and Beth Glass. 1992. "Categorization of Individuals on the Basis of Multiple Social Features." *Journal of Personality and Social Psychology* 62 (2): 207–218.

Steeh, Charlotte, and Maria Krysan. 1996. "The Polls—Trends: Affirmative Action and the Public, 1970–1995." *Public Opinion Quarterly* 60: 128–158.

Stein, Robert M., Stephanie Shirley Post, and Alison L. Rinden. 2000. "Reconciling Context and Contact Effects on Racial Attitudes." *Political Research Quarterly* 53: 285–303.

Sterling, T. D., W. L. Rosenbaum, and J. J. Weinkam. 1995. "Publication Decisions Revisited: The Effect of the Outcome of Statistical Tests on the Decision to Publish and Vice Versa." *American Statistician* 49: 108–112.

Stimson, James A. 1999. *Public Opinion in America: Moods, Cycles, and Swings.* 2nd ed. Boulder, Colo.: Westview Press.

Stoker, Laura. 2001. "Political Value Judgments." In *Citizens and Politics: Perspectives from Political Psychology*, James H. Kuklinski, ed., 433–468. Cambridge: Cambridge University Press.

Strope, Leigh. 1999a. "Lawmakers Don't Put Much Stock in Flag, Gambling Polls." Associated Press, September 27.

———. 1999b. "Hodges Presses for Flag Vote, Lifting of Boycott." Associated Press, November 18.

Sugrue, Thomas J. 1998. "The Tangled Roots of Affirmative Action." *American Behavioral Scientist* 41: 886–897.

———. 2004. "Affirmative Action from Below." *Journal of American History* 91 (1): 145–173.

———. 2005. *The Origins of the Urban Crisis.* Princeton, N.J.: Princeton University Press.

Taebel, Delbert A. 1975. "The Effect of Ballot Position on Electoral Success." *American Journal of Political Science* 19: 519–526.

Tajfel, Henri, M. G. Billig, R. P. Bundy, and Claude Flament. 1971. "Social Categorization and Intergroup Behaviour." *European Journal of Social Psychology* 1 (2): 149–178.

Tate, Katherine. 1993. *From Protest to Politics: The New Black Voters in American Elections.* Cambridge, Mass.: Harvard University Press.

Tate, Katherine. 2003. "Black Opinion on the Legitimacy of Racial Redistricting and Minority-Majority Districts." *American Political Science Review* 97: 45–56.

Tesler, Michael. 2012. "The Spillover of Racialization into Health Care: How President Obama Polarized Public Opinion by Racial Attitudes and Race." *American Journal of Political Science* 56 (3): 690–704.

Tesler, Michael, and David O. Sears. 2011. *Obama's Race: The 2008 Election and the Dream of a Post-Racial America.* Chicago: University of Chicago Press.

Thernstrom, Stephan, and Abigail Thernstrom. 1997. *America in Black and White: One Nation Indivisible.* New York: Simon and Schuster.

Toobin, Jeffrey. 2007. *The Nine: Inside the Secret World of the Supreme Court.* New York: Anchor Books.

Truman, Jennifer L., and Michael R. Rand. 2010. "Crime Victimization, 2009." US-DOJ Office of Justice Programs. http: //bjs.ojp.usdoj.gov.

Tversky, Amos, and Daniel Kahneman. 1981. "The Framing of Decisions and the Psychology of Choice." *Science*, n.s., 211 (4481): 453–458.

Underwood, Bill. 1997. "Ross Proposes Paying Race Riot Victims." *Tulsa World*, January 29.

U.S. Census Bureau. 2000. *Mapping Census 2000: The Geography of U.S. Diversity.* http: //www.census.gov.

———. 2007. "Income, Poverty, and Health Insurance Coverage in the United States." http: //www.census.gov/prod/2008pubs/p60-235.pdf.

———. 2010. "Detailed Years of School Completed by People 25 Years and Over by Sex, Age Groups, Race and Hispanic Origin." Current Population Survey, 2010 Annual Social and Economic Supplement. http: //www.census.gov.

———. 2011. "Statistical Abstract of the United States, 2011." Table 711. http: //www.census.gov.

U.S. Commission on Civil Rights. 2010. "Encouraging Minority Students to Pursue Science, Technology, Engineering, and Math Careers." Briefing Report. Washington, D.C.: Government Printing Office.

U.S. News and World Report. 2012. Top Public Schools. National Universities. http: //colleges.usnews.rankingsandreviews.com.

Walker, Jack L. 1966. "Ballot Forms and Voter Fatigue: An Analysis of the Office Block and Party Column Ballots." *Midwest Journal of Political Science* 10: 448–464.

Walker, Reagan. 1991. "Canada Urges Business to Buy Bond Issue." *Jackson Clarion-Ledger*, February 22.

Wenzel, Michael, Tyler G. Okimoto, Norman T. Feather, and Michael J. Platow. 2007. "Retributive and Restorative Justice." *Law and Human Behavior* 32 (5): 375–389.

Whitmire, Richard. 2010. Why Boys Fail: Saving Our Sons from an Educational System That's Leaving Them Behind. New York: American Management Association.

Williams, Daniel T. 1970, "The Lynching Records at Tuskegee Institute." In *Eight Negro Bibliographies*, Daniel T. Williams, ed. New York: Kraus Reprint Co.

Wilson, David C., David W. Moore, Patrick F. McKay, and Derek R. Avery. 2008. "Affirmative Action Programs for Women and Minorities: Expressed Support Affected by Question Order." *Public Opinion Quarterly* 72: 514–522.

Wilson, William Julius. 1990. "Race-Neutral Programs and the Democratic Coalition." *American Prospect* 1 (spring): 74–81.

———. 1999. "Affirming Opportunity." *American Prospect* 46 (September 1–October 1): 61–64.

———. 2010. *More than Just Race: Being Black and Poor in the Inner City.* New York: W. W. Norton.

Wolffe, Richard. 2009. *Renegade: The Making of a President.* New York: Broadway.

Wright, Gerald C., Jr. 1977. "Contextual Models of Electoral Behavior: The Southern Wallace Vote." *American Political Science Review* 71: 479–508.

Yankelovich, Daniel. 1991. *Coming to Public Judgment.* Syracuse, N.Y.: Syracuse University Press.

Zaller, John R. 1992. *The Nature and Origins of Mass Opinion.* New York: Cambridge University Press.

Zaller, John, and Stanley Feldman. 1992. "A Simple Theory of Survey Response: Answering Questions Versus Revealing Preferences." *American Journal of Political Science* 36: 579–616.

Zolper, Thomas. 1999. "Perception of Racial Bias: Whitman: Chief's Remarks 'Insensitive.'" *Bergen County Record*, March 2.

INDEX

ACKNOWLEDGMENTS

We are grateful to many people for their help, advice, insight, and encouragement on this project. It has been a great adventure, all the more so because of our network of colleagues and friends.

The foundation of this book is a series of experiments conducted through commercial and academic survey operations throughout the country. We received much advice on the construction of our experiments and relied completely upon the technical expertise of several organizations to realize them. For his help with the Mississippi and South Carolina experiments, we thank Brad Coker of Mason-Dixon Polling and Research Inc., Cliff Zukin, former director of the Star-Ledger/Eagleton-Rutgers Poll, and Mark DiCamillo, director of the California Field Poll, who facilitated the New Jersey and California experiments we report on in Chapter 4. Karen Clark of the Michigan State of the State Survey, based at Michigan State University, was extremely helpful as we developed and implemented the affirmative action experiments. In Oklahoma, our excellent partner was Katie Kimberling, formerly of the Oklahoma Poll at the University of Oklahoma.

Pieces of this manuscript have been presented in public and at conferences and workshops, and the guidance we have received from colleagues and friends has been invaluable. We thank Onur Bakiner, Jeffrey Berry, Jake Bowers, William "Sandy" Darity, Henry Flores, S. Michael Gaddis, Martin Gilens, Donald Green, Trevor Johnston, Kristyn Karl, Jeffrey Koch, Arthur Lupia, Rose McDermott, Tali Mendelberg, Rob Mickey, Justus Myers, Kent Portney, Molly Reynolds, Steve Teles, Rick Valelly, Claire Whitlinger, Cara Wong, and especially Melissa Nobles for their insight and willingness to share it. Thanks also to Jennifer Bailey, Lee Coffin, Rob Mickey, Nita Mukherjee, and Michael Sponhour of the South Carolina Budget and Control Board, who provided or helped us track down some important material and data. Dr. Ben Canada, former school superintendent in Jackson, Mississippi, provided us with special insight into the Jackson school bond plan, which is where this project first started.

The seed funding for the project came from a Russell Sage Foundation grant. The Tufts Faculty Research Awards Committee and the Office of the Dean of Arts and Sciences provided additional funds to put several experiments into the field. We are extremely grateful for this financial support and for the confidence it expressed in our ideas. We would be remiss if we did not also acknowledge Paul Sniderman, who organized and raised the resources for the original Multi-Investigator Surveys, which gave us an incredible opportunity to test some of our initial ideas. How lucky we are to count him as a friend and mentor.

We had the good fortune to connect with Rick Valelly, one of the editors of this series at University of Pennsylvania Press, at a critical moment in the process of writing this book. Rick's encouragement and desire to bring this manuscript to his editor colleagues convinced us that this was the right direction for us to move in. Our editor at University of Pennsylvania Press, Peter Agree, has delivered everything he promised. It is hard to overstate how valuable this has been and we are thankful. We also thank Sara Lickey, our copyeditor, and Noreen O'Connor, our production editor, who improved the readability and clarity of our prose.

Finally, we wish to acknowledge our families, whose support and love have sustained us through this process. Pamella Endo (Glaser) is the best spouse an academic could ever hope for. Catherine Ryan is the best mother a graduate student could ever hope for. Sadly, Joseph Ryan passed away shortly after we authors met, but the memory of his irrepressible curiosity and love of ideas is a fountain of inspiration. Alison and Jared Glaser have grown up as this book has grown up. They are a source of great pride. Amid demanding careers and the arrival of their beautiful daughter Ellia, Maryrose and Rockford Anthes-Weitz were gracious hosts for Tim during two extended trips to Boston. Thanks also to Charles and Fran Anthes-Washburn, Brian and Leona Fagan, Brian and Amy Glaser Gage, Judy Glaser, Jeffrey and Lori Glaser Korn, and William Washburn. They have always been there, and we are incredibly fortunate for it.